Praise for My Marri~

"Long a trusted source for the media on sustaining a successful marriage, Leah Fisher now brings us a kind of "Eat, Pray, Love" for the faithfully married set. This book is a feast of wisdom for anyone struggling to balance midlife self-expression with marital commitment, and it is essential reading for spouses considering a breakup as balm for a restless soul. Leah knows not only how to counsel couples on marriage—she demonstrates first-hand what it takes to sustain a vibrant, lifelong union.

—*Sue Shellenbarger*, former *Work & Family* columnist
for *The Wall Street Journal*

"Leah Fisher tells a tale of two fascinating journeys. The first involves a negotiation with her husband that re-shapes their marriage, making room for a year of solo global travel. The second journey includes charmingly described accounts of living in a series of Asian and Latin American cultures. Both parts of this unusual exploration are beautifully written. *My Marriage Sabbatical: A Memoir of Solo Travel and Lasting Love* has much to teach us about the rewarding but challenging opportunities for partners to follow their dreams within long-term marriages."

—*Carolyn and Philip Cowan*, Directors of
the Becoming a Family Project, and authors
of *When Partners Become Parents*

"With the insights of a long-time couples' therapist, the zest of a woman in her sixties pursuing her dreams, and the sensitivity of a wife still committed to her marriage of many decades, Leah Fisher inspires us by sharing her solo global adventures in a later life "gap year." From Costa Rica and Guatemala to Colombia, Cuba, Java, and Bali, Fisher combines community service with exploring new cultures and making friends, young and older. She collaborates skillfully with her husband who opts to stay home and keep working but meets her abroad every few months so that their relationship stays strong and vibrant. *My Marriage Sabbatical: A Memoir of Solo Travel and Lasting Love* is an entertaining read and a blueprint for readers ready to address their own aspirations."

—*Elizabeth Fishel*, author of *The Men in Our Lives,* and *Getting To 30: A Parent's Guide to the 20-Something Years*

"Leah Fisher has written a book that will touch your heart, open your eyes, and excite your imagination. Her journey is one that many women would love to take. She and her husband reach an agreement to be apart for a year, as she brings a deeply meaningful dream to life. Read this book; you may discover a dream of your own!"

—*Lynne Twist*, cofounder of the Pachamama Alliance and author of *The Soul of Money*

"You are amazing at playing with me."

—*Ryu de Leon*, age 9, note to his grandmother on Mothers' Day

My
Marriage
Sabbatical

A MEMOIR OF SOLO TRAVEL
AND LASTING LOVE

Leah Fisher

SHE WRITES PRESS

Published 2025
Printed in the United States of America
Print ISBN: 978-1-64742-734-4
E-ISBN: 978-1-64742-735-1
Library of Congress Control Number: 2024917351

For information, address:
She Writes Press
1569 Solano Ave #546
Berkeley, CA 94707

Interior Design by Tabitha Lahr

She Writes Press is a division of SparkPoint Studio, LLC.

Names and identifying characteristics have been changed to protect the privacy of certain individuals.

For "Charley"

"Let there be spaces in your togetherness . . ."
—*Kahlil Gibran*

"The traveler sees what he sees,
The tourist sees what he has come to see."
—*Gilbert K. Chesterton*

"When you set out for Ithaca,
Ask that your way be long,
Full of adventure,
Full of instruction."
—*C. P. Cavafy*

Contents

CHAPTER 1

Shaking Up the Empty Nest

ARIZONA and CALIFORNIA

"*Enough is ENOUGH!*"

Shouting at the top of my lungs, I deliver my notice shortly after sunrise, surrounded by saguaros, on a deserted path in the Catalina Mountains.

As my words echo through the Arizona canyon, I am startled by the force of my explosion. The sudden rush of energy is so exhilarating that I place my hands on my knees, bend forward, and roar again:

"*I have grieved long enough!*"

Five years ago, during a heartbreaking two-year span, my father died and both children left home. Thoroughly walloped, I grew accustomed to living with a tamped-down mood, capably doing whatever each day required while feeling just a little sad and making the best of long evenings waiting for my husband, Charley, to come home.

Reflecting on my outburst in the Arizona desert, I sense that something is about to shift. I'm not sure what, but I can certainly recognize a sign when I see one.

A week later, I am back home in California. It is almost 10:00 p.m. Charley is working late again. My own workday as a psychotherapist is long over. I've eaten dinner alone for the third night in a row. Not *dinner*, really; what I do on evenings like this is more like grazing.

Charley's pattern of long workdays, nighttime professional meetings, and out-of-town conferences has been an ongoing source of friction throughout our twenty-seven-year marriage. His hectic schedule made sense during his medical training. But long after his psychiatry practice was established and flourishing, his intense eleven- to fourteen-hour days continued.

A friend and I used to ponder in jest, "Do you think it's possible Charley has a secret second family?"

In a way, it is true. My husband *is* having an affair.

With his work!

After our son and daughter were born, the conflict between Charley's professional ambitions and my yearning for a more equitable relationship and a close-knit family life escalated.

The problem was loneliness. I missed my husband, and I yearned for him to spend more time with us. I wanted him to be more engaged with our children and our home. And I wanted something else . . . something I couldn't quite identify and wouldn't be able to put into words for many years.

Charley and I are deeply attached despite our ongoing difficulties. I married a man who is basically good-natured: cheerful, courteous, and respectful toward our children and me. I enjoy his company when he is at home. He is an attentive listener; we have a satisfying sex life; and when we can get away, he is a wonderful travel companion. But our attachment could never assuage the tension between Charley's professional ambitions and my dream of a warm homelife and a close relationship. It didn't take away the sting of living with a trade-off we both hated. Charley proceeded to do exactly what he wanted while stoically tolerating my resentment and anger.

My frustration about Charley's lack of time and involvement remained undiminished. Over the years, I tried to influence him by means of eloquent explanations, polite requests, and fervent pleas; also by nagging, criticizing, and periodically having nasty meltdowns. None of it resulted in change. Instead, I settled into part-time professional work and hired loving caregivers to help us make a warm home for the children.

———

It's 10:15. My thoughts drift back to our kids' departures from home. When our son, Mischa, left for college, followed a year later by our daughter, Shahla, I fell into an immense chasm of loss. First, there was the concrete loss of their company: their humor, energy, music, friends, even their clutter. But there was the additional loss of future possibilities. I had to permanently let go of the hope that someday Charley would cut back his hours so our family could enjoy evenings together and we could have the cozy, nurturing home I'd always wanted.

———

By now it's 10:30. I am sitting in front of the computer, longing for a marriage where dinner is a shared event and an evening together lasts longer than the forty-five minutes between Charley's return and our going to sleep. On a whim, I click on Craigslist, the online bulletin board for anything and everything. I type "roommates wanted" and read a few ads for house shares . . . *too scary*. Then I notice a category for "short-term rentals in shared houses," click, and find this ad:

Come share our sweet, cozy Berkeley home. Our house is filled with houseplants and flowers, music and massage. We love to cook, do yoga, and garden. We are twenty-five-and twenty-seven-year-old women. One of us is a yoga teacher and massage therapist; the other works for a nonprofit doing youth philanthropy. We are looking for a twenty-something woman or gentle man to join our warm and happy household for a month or longer. Email and tell us about yourself.

My heart starts racing. Among my favorite and most joyful activities are gardening, singing, yoga, and massage. A month-long sublet would involve no ongoing obligation; I wouldn't have to inconvenience or deceive anyone. It could provide the perfect experiment. I could find out if my fantasy of people spending an evening together, sharing cooking and eating and making a home beautiful, is just that—a fantasy—or if it might indeed fill the gaping hole I feel so often in our empty house.

Without a second thought, I shoot back a reply:

I too love yoga, and music and gardening. I am quite interested in a one-month sublet in your communal household. However, I am not twenty-something. I am fifty-nine. I am married and live in Orinda with a husband who works long hours. I would like to have company the three to four evenings a week that he works late, and I'd like to explore ways to make our homelife cozier and more enjoyable.

PS Before you freak out about my age, please consider this: if all goes well, someday you will feel very much the way you do now, only you will have wrinkles and others will see you as old.

A week has passed with no response to my inquiry about the room for rent. I'm not exactly surprised. The roommate-seeking girls were probably turned off as soon as they read "I am fifty-nine." I put it out of my mind.

A few days later, I receive an email from Serena saying that she and her housemate, Colleen, are intrigued by my response and would like to meet me. So, in the darkness of an early winter evening, I drive down an unfamiliar street until I find the address I'm looking for. Here it is—a tired-looking two-story brown shingle house, one of many that surround the UC Berkeley campus. Carefully climbing the gray lamplit steps, I notice the peeling paint exposing remnants of previous colors. The banister feels a little rickety. Standing on the porch, I hesitate. *What in the world am I doing?* I lift the chilly knocker and rap on the door.

A beautiful, doe-eyed, dark-haired young woman opens the door. This is Serena. She leads me through a plant-filled, futon-furnished living room to the kitchen and introduces me to Colleen, who is as blond and adorable as Serena is dark-haired and dignified. They offer me tea, and I feel quite comfortable as we chat, share stories, and ask one another questions.

Eventually, Serena sets her mug down gently on the 1950s-era red Formica table. "Colleen and I are curious to know why you want to live in our house when you already have a house of your own." She continues bravely and as diplomatically as possible. "We wonder if there might be something going on in your marriage."

"My marriage is OK," I assure them. "However, my husband, Charley, works crazy hours. I recently brought up the idea of a housemate. But it's been decades since I've lived in a group house, so I thought this would be a chance to experience it again. Also, I'd like my husband to find out how it feels to be the one coming home to an empty house."

My explanation makes sense to the two young women. Colleen says, "We both have boyfriends, so we get it." Serena adds, "I admire that you and your husband still work on your relationship after being married for so long." At the end of our visit, they warmly invite me to move in.

———

The next evening, I tell Charley over dinner that I have something important to discuss with him. When I have his attention, I explain that I am planning to rent a room for a month in a group house. "That way, on the nights you work late, I can have the company of housemates."

Charley is speechless. In all the years I have known him, I've never seen my husband at a loss for words, but he is now. When he finally collects himself, he says frostily, "Are you leaving me?"

"Absolutely not," I answer. "Really, this is just what I said. Any night you come home at dinnertime, I'll be here. I'll be here on the weekends. And the girls say you are welcome to stay over any night you want."

"Do you still love me?"

"Oh, yes. This isn't *against* you, Charley; it is *for* me. I'm trying to figure out what I need to be happy."

Charley says nothing more, and soon we go to bed.

At four o'clock in the morning, Charley awakens me, angry. "I am intensely upset," he says in an accusatory voice.

"Don't try to scare me with your anger," I respond, feeling threatened but trying not to let it show.

"I'm not angry, I'm upset. Guys can sound angry when they are upset. And what you told me tonight has me *extremely* upset."

Of course he is upset; never in our marriage have I done something this unilateral. I lie on my side of the bed, silent for a long time. Then I speak, carefully but firmly. "Charley, I am finished ignoring my needs and my dreams to protect you from your intense feelings. I am *so* finished with it."

Charley is silent; I roll over and go back to sleep.

———

I move into the Blake Street house the next Monday evening. My room is the middle bedroom on the second floor. It already has a futon bed, a little nightstand, and a dresser. I have loaded my station wagon with some bedding, a small rug, and a favorite reading lamp I made in my twenties from a brass hookah. I've also brought a little wooden meditation altar—a childhood carpentry project of Mischa's—along with my meditation cushion, a journal, and a piece of orange batik fabric to hang over the windows. These plus some toiletries and a change of clothes will be sufficient.

Serena, Colleen, and Serena's boyfriend, Arturo, help me unpack my car and set up my room. I find a perfect, single white lily in a tall vase on the dresser, a welcoming gesture. After I unpack, the four of us settle into the small kitchen. The stove and refrigerator look to be forty years old; the linoleum floor looks even older. Serena and Arturo eat dinner while Colleen and I drink tea. We talk and laugh, getting acquainted. It feels sweet. There is no TV in sight and no computer. The phone rings only once all evening and goes unanswered. No one jumps up to check email, do paperwork, or study for the next day. Clearly, the action takes place *in* this house, not primarily outside it.

We wish each other goodnight and proceed upstairs. Just as I am settling into my comfortable bed to sleep, snuggling under my yellow flannel sheets and soft down quilt, nestling my head into the pillow, the house starts shaking.

Earthquake! My lifelong terror kicks in. *Not in this rickety two-story house. I wanted to shake things up, not to die! These old boards are probably infested with termites. Is a house this old even bolted to the foundation?* The house shakes gently, rhythmically.

Gradually, I recognize the motion for what it is—the rhythm of young lovemaking. I smile with relief. In about ten minutes, there is silence.

After my first night at the Blake Street house, I spend an afternoon at home. I enjoy a few minutes weeding the garden in the sun, then spend hours indoors. I think about the serene simplicity of my sparsely furnished room in Berkeley. At home, I feel trapped inside my house by paperwork. I look longingly outside, but I have calls to return, bills to pay, and appointments to schedule. Soon the afternoon is gone.

When I talk to Serena about this experience a few evenings later, she promptly identifies the problem. "We've got to set clear boundaries." She may be young, but she's right. "We need to be selective, to protect home and evenings as a sanctuary." When Serena and Colleen come home at night, they are home. No more work. It is time for relaxation, conversation, and preparation for rest.

On Friday, I return home to Charley. We're together for three nights. I remain loving, cheerful, and fully available to him. He is starting to believe that I'm not trying to punish him or get even. Nevertheless, he doesn't ask about the other house or my housemates, and he ignores all my invitations to come by or sleep over. But at least he isn't angry, prickly, or defensive.

One night, when I enter the Blake Street house, I find Colleen in the living room giving a massage to a friend. The aroma of fragrant massage oil and the glow of candlelight are embracing. The focus in this household is on physical well-being and sensory pleasure: healthy eating, flowers, music, and massages. I realize that at home with Charley, I want some of our evenings devoted to nurturing our bodies and delighting our senses. *Minds* are just fine, but I don't want to put all my attention there.

The month flies by. I am enjoying my cozy, uncomplicated evenings at the Blake Street house. I love Charley's company when he's at home. And I relish not having to spend endless evenings alone.

As my time at Blake Street draws toward an end, Colleen and Serena have still not found a permanent renter. I am happy with our arrangement and propose staying on for a few more weeks while they continue to look. My housemates are enthusiastic; Charley is noncommittal.

The experiment ends abruptly during my first bonus week. When I arrive after work on Thursday evening, Serena greets me at the door with news. "We've found a renter!" I am momentarily stunned, then delighted for them that their search is over. Serena brings me into the kitchen where Colleen and a sweet-faced young man are having tea. Colleen introduces me to Rob. He seems gentle and open and easygoing—exactly what she and Colleen were hoping for. As we chat at the kitchen table, Serena asks Rob when he'd like to move in. "If it's OK," he responds, "I'd like to move in right away. I could use a place to sleep tonight." It is an awkward moment for my housemates. They look at me uncomfortably until I ease the tension with humor. "Well, you're in luck. You need a place to sleep, and I happen to have *two* places to sleep. You can certainly have the room."

So, just as quickly as they had helped me unpack and settle into that room five weeks before, my housemates help me repack, and I am home in Orinda by the time Charley returns from work at 10:00 p.m. He is surprised to see me, but by now he is getting used to surprises.

Serena emails me from her work the next day.

It felt empty in the house after you left. I found myself looking forward to seeing you yesterday, then POOF! Everything had shifted. These rapid shifts can feel a bit ungrounding, but this one does not feel so much that way. It feels right, although momentarily my mind is reeling from its swiftness. I am grateful that we've had the chance to get to know each other. Blessings to you, Leah.
Serena

It was an abrupt ending for me as well. I am at home again; left to distill what I've learned from this experience. And I realize that I've learned a lot. I learned that I can be audacious . . . sometimes very audacious. I found out that Charley can tolerate my shaking up our empty nest if he's sure it is not against him. At the Blake Street house, Colleen and Serena showed me that nourishment of the senses and attentive care of the body are essential ingredients for a peaceful, happy evening. I discovered that some of what makes me lonely is the amount of time that I, too, spend working. I miss *me* at home as well as missing Charley. I found out that in certain ways, I'm braver and more creative than when I was younger. And I discovered that a big part of the pleasure in having an adventure is knowing I will be returning to Charley at the end of it.

Soon after this experiment, Charley announces that he has modified his work schedule and will be coming home an hour earlier on both Monday and Thursday nights. He hastens to assure me that this change has nothing whatever to do with my moving out. I wisely keep my mouth shut and my thoughts to myself. Regardless of how it came about, I am delighted with the result.

Later, reflecting on my experience, I marvel at how my ideas about marriage and "happily ever after" have changed over the years. When I was younger, I thought *grown-up* was a destination. I didn't realize it would be an ongoing process of discovery, of daring to reveal more and more of who we really are. When Charley and I got married, I had no idea that our marriage might need to be negotiated and renegotiated at various times for us to live "happily ever after."

It seems that one of those times has arrived.

CHAPTER 2

Awakening the Dreamer

ECUADOR

We never planned on taking a trip into the Amazon jungle. It was more like the rainforest came and wrapped its vines around us. The first tendril appeared at a book event featuring Lynne Twist, author of *The Soul of Money*. The title struck a chord. I didn't know this Lynne Twist or what she would discuss, but I was intrigued.

Money is consistently one of the top areas of conflict among spouses and is often the reason couples come to my office for therapy. Their financial situations cover the whole income spectrum, from poverty to great wealth. Money conflicts, although seemingly about finances, often reflect the *meaning and purpose* of money to each person. If money represents enjoyment and generosity to one spouse but security and a rainy-day rescue to the other, disagreements about spending versus saving are almost inevitable. Then, throw in a tone of moral superiority, and a disagreement can quickly escalate into a fight.

In the past, Charley and I have had some nasty fights over money. I hated that Charley wouldn't make a budget or track income and outflow. What he thought of as cash flow problems, I considered irresponsibility. He thought I was too anxious; I thought he was too complacent.

"What would it feel like to you if we were to run out of money?" he asked one day.

"It would feel like falling off a cliff."

"Interesting. To me, it would feel like getting my shoes muddy."

⎯⎯⎯

I call Charley at work. "There's an event tonight for a new book called *The Soul of Money*. Would you like to go with me?"

"Sure, why not?" Our evening together turns out to be full of surprises. As the beautiful, gracious woman is introduced, Charley turns to me and whispers, "I think I know her. She had a different last name then, but I think she went to my high school in Chicago." Before he can say more, the presentation begins.

The Soul of Money is a book about philanthropy. "In a successful money relationship," Lynne Twist explains, "money flows through our lives, becoming an expression of our deepest passions, values, and commitments." Offering a personal example, the author describes her work with an indigenous tribe in the Ecuadorian Amazon. She and her husband, Bill, founded the Pachamama Alliance to partner with the Achuar people in protecting their rainforest home from destruction by the petroleum industry. Their organization offers trips to the Amazon to help North Americans comprehend the importance of the rainforests and the present threat to the planet. In passing, Lynne mentions that the Achuar are a dream culture. Their nightly dreams inform and direct their daily lives.

Charley turns to me, his eyes wide. I know what he is thinking. Dreams fascinate him; they are a valuable part of psychoanalytic work. Charley and I exchange a meaningful glance. Our wordless message is "Let's go for it!"

After the talk, when we reach the front of the line where Lynne is signing books, Charley asks if by any chance she had been the homecoming queen in his high school graduating class. Lynne lifts her head in surprise and looks at him. "Why yes, as a matter of fact, I was. Who are you?"

Charley introduces himself, and Lynne looks at him thoughtfully. "Weren't you one of our class valedictorians?"

"Why yes, as a matter of fact, I was."

———

How odd that the popular homecoming queen and the nerdy brainiac whose paths scarcely crossed in high school should get reacquainted forty years later. And that is how Charley and I find ourselves at nearly ten thousand feet above sea level one August morning, adapting to the altitude of Quito, Ecuador, and waiting to meet the sixteen other people with whom we will journey into the Amazon jungle.

In two tiny planes, our newly formed group flies for an hour past the last visible road. From above, the jungle looks like a vast broccoli forest threaded with brown ribbons of river. Our destination is Kapawi Ecolodge, located in Achuar territory. When we descend and come to a bumpy halt on the dirt airstrip, a cluster of excited children race toward the plane. Several muscular young men wearing dramatic red face paint in geometric patterns greet us and carry our luggage from the airstrip to the riverbank. From there, two motorized canoes bring us to Kapawi Lodge. A wooden boardwalk extends from the muddy river to the main building of the lodge. There we find shelves of tall, black rubber boots. These will be our footwear throughout our stay in the rainforest. We are grateful for the rubber boots during our daily hikes in the humid jungle.

On the third day of our journey, the group travels by canoe to a neighboring Achuar village to meet with the community leader.

Welcoming visitors to an Achuar home involves serving a drink called *chicha*. It is a fermented beverage made from manioc root, cooked in river water, and mixed with female saliva. Each day the women dig up, boil, and chew large quantities of manioc root, crushing and tenderizing the woody fibers with their saliva and then spitting it back into the pot. The mixture is then left to ferment. Charley will tell our friends after we get home, "Chicha tastes as good as it sounds."

As we sit on long benches facing the community leader, the women serve us chicha in clay bowls that they baked in the fire and painted with geometric patterns. I notice they avoid eye contact with any of the men in our group. Lynne explains that Achuar women do not make eye contact with men other than their spouses. Here is one more custom for us to remember and observe.

While we sip (or pretend to sip) our chicha, we introduce ourselves to the leader. Bill and Lynne have told us that our visits and respectful interest encourage the Achuar's pride in their culture and their traditional way of life. It helps counteract the disparaging messages they receive from the outside world: that indigenous people are uncivilized, dirty, and ignorant.

Sitting in the village leader's open-air house, we ask questions. Two translators ferry our questions back and forth: English to Spanish, Spanish to Achuar, and back again. A man from Kentucky asks, "What do you believe is important to teach your children, and what do you want for your children?" The leader answers, "We want our children to be strong and courageous. We teach our sons to hunt."

His response awakens memories of our own son, Mischa, at age four. Enthralled with toy guns and sticks and ropes and slingshots, his play involved shooting, throwing, and tying. He slept with his toy rifle. But here's where the similarity ends. While parents and preschool teachers in our culture are laboring to teach four-year-old boys how to sit still and raise their hands,

Achuar fathers are teaching theirs to hunt, track, and use a blowgun. As I listen to the leader's answer, I grow more curious about this culture and more reflective about my own.

One of the lovely things about foreign travel is our openness to new experiences. When Lynne and Bill invite us to participate in a sacred shamanic healing ceremony using ayahuasca, Charley and I are among the first who say yes. "To prepare," Lynne informs us, "you will need to fast for twenty-four hours. Then we will hike in silence for three hours through the jungle to the shaman's village, where the ceremony will take place." She emphasizes the sacred nature of the ceremony we are about to experience. One group member innocently asks how long the effects of the powerful hallucinogen will last, and Lynne replies, "For the rest of your life, I hope."

Our long trek on narrow trails leaves us tired and sweaty. We finally arrive at a clearing planted with banana trees and square patches of manioc. The shaman's house has no walls. It is simply a woven roof on stilts with a dirt floor below. The "private" half of the large open space has a family sleeping platform. Our own sleeping quarters have already been set up: eighteen little mosquito-netted catacombs side by side. Through the netting, I can see that each contains an inflatable mat, a sheet, and a pillow.

"Ayahuasca is made by combining and boiling the bark of one tree and the leaves from another," explains Lynne. "The taste is bitter and unpleasant, so it's best to drink it quickly." Just as I'm wondering *how* unpleasant, she adds: "Ayahuasca can make you nauseous. If it does, it's fine to throw up anywhere except within the shaman's house. The soil will quickly absorb it."

At nightfall, we sit on low wooden stools in a semicircle around the shaman. Fourteen of us have chosen to participate in the ayahuasca ceremony; the remaining four will serve as helpers. Charley is seated on the stool to my left. The shaman chants over the large kettle of ayahuasca on the table in front of him. Then he calls us up one by one. When it is my turn, I bow to the shaman, take the bowl, and down the thick brown liquid. It is bitter, though not as bad as I had feared. Still, I wouldn't want to serve it to guests.

Even before the last person has drunk from the shaman's bowl, I need to vomit. For the sake of those still waiting, I vow to keep out of the bushes until everyone has taken their turn. I keep my promise, but just barely. After throwing up more than I thought possible, I return to the shelter of the shaman's house. Almost immediately, I feel dizzy and heavy . . . too heavy to stay upright. In the dark, I find a log bench beside our netted beds. Everything is whirling as I lower myself onto the bench. I feel my back pressing against the hard surface. Maybe I can control the dizziness if I'm careful not to move. After a while, I tentatively open my eyes. The Amazon night sky is completely sequined with stars. I search for the Big Dipper, but instead I find the unfamiliar constellations of the southern hemisphere. I lie cemented to the bench, eyes closed, but soon force myself to stand. I stagger jerkily toward the bushes, kneel on the dirt, and resume violently throwing up. Finally, I grope my way back to the bench. I will walk to the bushes many times during this long night.

At some point, Lynne comes to assist me. She holds my head, stroking my hair and my back while I throw up. She asks one of the helpers to bring a banana leaf so I can rest on the ground just outside the shaman's house. Lying face down on the ground, fully aware of my stonelike heaviness and unable to move, I wonder if perhaps this is what dying will be like. I feel connected to the earth as I lie there on my stomach. I'm not scared, just completely removed from the activity of living. Now I understand why ayahuasca is called the "vine of death." Like an arrow, truth pierces my lifelong fear of death, a fear that conceals the tenacious hope that if I'm just good enough and sufficiently vigilant, I might be excused from mortality. Ayahuasca brings me face-to-face with the powerful reality: someday, I truly *will* be dying.

Lynne comes to my side. "You are purging whatever you need to release." Later that night, when there is nothing left to purge, she will help me into my little sleeping catacomb.

Charley is sweet during the night. Lying next to me, he reaches through the netting to touch my hand and asks, "Are you OK?" I know he is near, but I am too deeply elsewhere to respond.

When we return home, incredulous friends will ask, "Why did you do it? Why did you want to take ayahuasca?"

"I suppose because I've never done it before." It's true. In going to the Amazon, Charley and I weren't seeking to be healed from anything except, perhaps, our ignorance. Our journey to the rainforest led us to question who is informed and who is ignorant. Every Achuar person knows trees have spirits and must be honored and protected, while "educated" people consider trees mere resources to be exploited until the earth lies gasping for breath.

In the morning, Charley tells me about his vision. "I was looking at all those stars in the night sky. Then I saw the constellations of the southern hemisphere embrace the constellations of the northern hemisphere." Charley is delighted with his vision. It perfectly portrays what will soon become an ongoing research interest: understanding the use and meaning of dreams among the Achuar and their relevance to psychotherapy practice in the northern hemisphere. I feel very close to my husband and proud of him, too.

The following day, we fly out of the rainforest in the same tiny planes. Leaving the humidity of the jungle, we cross the equator to the cold and windy towering mountains of the Andes. After a few welcome days of rest, Lynne invites us to visit another shaman, a man who works with fire. After getting assurance that we would not be ingesting *anything*, most of our now tight-knit group sign on. It is not until we are filing off the bus in front of Don Esteban's house that our guide and translator, Juan Gabriel, quietly informs us that we will need to take off our clothing for this next ceremony.

Don Esteban is an elderly shaman who heals by invoking the fiery power of three gigantic volcanoes that surround the town of Otavalo. When he is ready to begin, he puts on a tall headdress of colorful feathers. One by one, we sit in front of the old man while his son—also a shaman—passes an unlit candle all over and around our body. He then hands the candle to his father and the weathered shaman examines it carefully, reading our energy and making a diagnosis. After that, he lights our candle and addresses us in Quichua, the indigenous language. His son translates from Quichua to Spanish, and then Juan Gabriel translates from Spanish into English.

When it is my turn to sit in front of Don Esteban, he studies my candle and then looks at me. "Your energy is very positive and has been so since birth. However, your energy is out of balance, perhaps due to boredom or anger." *Or maybe both*, I think. Don Esteban looks again at the candle and adds, "Also, it is your destiny to be with your husband." (He has not been told that Charley is present, sitting on a bench across the room.)

The younger shaman next goes around the circle and examines each person's palms. There are fifteen of us in the room. After looking at Charley's hands, he turns back toward me in surprise. I hear him ask Juan Gabriel if we are *esposos*, husband and wife. Receiving confirmation, he beckons me over. "Look, these lines are the same." The elder shaman reiterates that it is clearly our destiny to be together in marriage. Given my perpetual tendency to doubt myself and question my choices, I am intrigued. How much kinder to believe Charley and I are together by destiny than by mistake.

When it is Charley's turn to have Don Esteban read his candle, the shaman tells him, "You are a healer. However, you do not heal with your hands; you heal with your vision." I am impressed; it is a good description of a psychiatrist. But nothing prepares me for what he says next. "The path you are walking is a good path, but it is a narrow one. To walk the path of matrimony and to fulfill your destiny, you must broaden your path." I am astonished. Now *how* could he know that?

Next comes a cleansing ceremony guaranteed to make a skeptic's eyes roll. Juan Gabriel instructs us to remove all our clothes and line up on the cold cement floor facing the shaman. *What have I gotten myself into?* After a moment of hesitation, I take off my warm gray poncho newly purchased in the Otavalo market and pile my trekking clothes onto the bench. The ingredients for the ceremony lie on the shaman's table: candles, liquor, flowers, cinnamon, perfume, and cigarettes. The son fills his mouth with *trago*, an alcoholic drink akin to cheap rum. Then, with a powerful exhalation, he sprays the liquor all over our naked bodies. *Ouch!* The alcohol is freezing cold as it hits my skin. Standing barefoot and naked on the cold cement, I am not embarrassed. My experience is one of sensations, not thoughts or judgments. Charley, also naked, is right beside me. I am grateful for his stalwart presence. I wonder what he is feeling.

"*Chungo, chungo, chungo,*" chants the shaman as he invokes the spirits of the three volcanoes: Imbabura, Cotacachi, and Mojanda. Meanwhile, his assistant blows mouthfuls of *trago* at us through a lighted candle. This creates splendid balls of fire that land just short of our shivering naked bodies. Next, he gives us cinnamon and flower petals to rub over our now-soaked limbs. Finally, he blows tobacco smoke onto each of our open palms, our foreheads, and the very tops of our heads. He distributes knitted woolen caps to "hold in the healing energy" and instructs us not to remove the caps or bathe for twenty-four hours. Charley and I wear the thick, striped woolen caps to dinner and notice that all our fellow travelers are wearing theirs as well.

A narrow path can be limiting. Or boring. However, there is nothing boring about being with Charley now. Our shared path is growing broader before our very eyes.

CHAPTER 3

Reviving the Dream

ECUADOR

I know better than to spring things on Charley. Periodically, I've mentioned my wish to travel for an extended time. Occasionally, I've said, "I feel like change is in the air." I have been preparing Charley for something, even though neither of us knows exactly what.

———

Casa Mojanda is an ecolodge high in the Andes, designed and built by an Ecuadorian man and his American wife. The rustic main lodge, with its breathtaking views of a volcano and the cluster of white *casitas* dotting the slope above Otavalo, is this couple's dream come true. Our Pachamama group has come here to enjoy the last few days of our journey.

The altitude is so extreme that just walking the short distance from our casita to the lodge leaves me winded. While Charley goes for a short walk, I listen to Inca music in the lodge. The hollow sound of panpipes resonates in my chest, as it always does. The lodge's owner enters the room and offers to show me their organic garden. "Much of the lodge's food is grown here," she tells me with pride. "We also have a charitable foundation that supports a local kindergarten, and we sponsor six-month internships for volunteers."

Then and there, I know what I want to do.

———

The idea of taking a stretch of time to explore the world, live in a different culture, and find ways to be of service has been an enduring dream. It first emerged when I was about to graduate from college, wondering what to do next.

The Peace Corps was in its heyday. The best and the brightest among my classmates were applying, some as newly married couples and some on their own. I, too, filled out a Peace Corps application, but sadly, I wasn't accepted. The main reason I wasn't accepted was because I never mailed in my application! I was terrified of going so far away—to some underdeveloped foreign country, completely alone, for two whole years. Instead, I went to graduate school and studied social work. It wasn't scary, but it sure was uninspiring. Two years later, I watched friends return from the Peace Corps transformed by their experiences. They returned with a broader global perspective, a clearer sense of purpose, and an enviable supply of confidence. Over the years, whenever someone would mention the Peace Corps, I'd be flooded with stinging regret.

———

My dream of unstructured exploration and foreign travel continued to beckon periodically. I had tastes of it from time to time, and they were always delicious. In my midtwenties, while vacationing in Maui with my best friend, we stopped at the funky

Pioneer Inn in Lahaina. It was sunset. On the hotel's wraparound porch were clusters of young men in shorts and girls wearing sarongs and flip-flops. They were drinking beer and hanging out happily. It was a typical relaxed evening in paradise, and I was riveted. This was precisely what I yearned for. I wanted to be one of those young women who came to Hawaii and stayed. Like them, I wanted to be relaxed and free, with nothing to do at the end of the day except stand around on the porch of the Pioneer Inn, sip beer, and watch the sun slip into the sea.

Instead, I went back to my job at Planned Parenthood, where I was helping to develop a pregnancy and abortion counseling service. It was the late 1960's, and I was engrossed and stimulated, an active participant in what would later be called the women's liberation movement. I loved my work and the engaged sisterhood, although it didn't address the passionate impulse that emerged in Hawaii. My travel dreams receded into the background.

A year later, I received a postcard from a college classmate. My good friend Brad *had* mailed in his Peace Corps application. He had volunteered for two years in Honduras and was now living in Central America. On the front of the postcard was a photograph of a breathtaking lake surrounded by towering volcanoes. On the back was a cryptic message—"Paradise is alive and well"— and a roughly drawn map leading to Lake Atitlán in Guatemala.

That summer, I negotiated a month's leave from my clinic and flew to Guatemala to visit Brad and his girlfriend. We met at the airport in Guatemala City and took one of those red, crazily painted public buses to the tiny Maya pueblo of Panajachel on the shore of Lake Atitlán. (At that time, Panajachel was a little-known indigenous *pueblito* in the highlands bearing no resemblance to the noisy, sprawling tourist mecca that is present-day "Pana.")

What a magical month. I stayed with my friends in their small, blue, rented stucco house on one of the dirt paths leading to the lake. We spent our days swimming, soaking in the hot springs where the Maya came to bathe, visiting neighboring villages, or just sitting on a log at night eating popcorn and watching heat lightning over the lake. I especially enjoyed walking through the little pueblo and watching Brad charm the indigenous children with his playful humor. They followed him like the Pied Piper.

That visit to Lake Atitlán became the template for my vision of global travel. It included settling into a cozy home base, wandering at will, finding companionship, exploring in a leisurely way, and making do with very little.

———

Charley and I, along with the rest of the Pachamama group, are making our way down the steep mountain toward the market in Otavalo. It is early in the morning. The fog is thick, the grass is damp, the air is thin, and the mountains are magnificent. Charley and I are walking a bit apart from the others.

"Charley," I begin. "There is something I want to discuss with you. I just found out there's an internship program here at Casa Mojanda. It has so much of what I love: living in community, learning Spanish, growing food, and helping young children. I think I want to apply for it, *with* you if you'd come, or perhaps on my own."

Charley listens respectfully, and I feel the delight of having his full attention.

"I can hear your excitement," he says warmly, "and I want to know all your thoughts, but let's save any real negotiation for later in our trip."

I feel a twinge of exasperation, but it quickly passes. We are really going to talk about this, not just hint at it. I take Charley's arm and pull him close. I feel joyfully serene and, at the same time, giddy with excitement. This important conversation is going to happen. Arm in arm, we rejoin the group and continue our invigorating walk into the market town of Otavalo.

CHAPTER 4

Love, Honor, and Negotiate

ECUADOR

As a couple, Charley and I have learned to be world-class negotiators. A friend married to a very accommodating, easygoing fellow once remarked, "You and Charley negotiate *everything*. It must be exhausting." Perhaps so, but for us, it has been important. We are both strong-willed individuals, each of us possessed with a well-developed sense of entitlement. What would you expect from an only child—a boy born after multiple miscarriages—married to a woman who was her father's favored child? How could we *not* have a complicated marriage?

Charley and I met when I was twenty-eight and he was twenty-six. We dated briefly, and then I moved on. I stayed single and seeking. Turning thirty came as a shock. I wanted babies so much I could taste it. When Charley again showed interest, I was ready to give this awkward, earnest young man another try.

As we got to know each other, I was alternately friendly and standoffish. That changed on the weekend Charley took me canoe camping. Early one Saturday morning, he picked me up with a green wooden canoe strapped on top of his battered, sunflower-yellow Datsun. Our destination was Cherry Lake, a pristine body of water near Yosemite. During the long, hot drive through the central valley to the Sierras, I chattered, telling Charley more than I ever had about my growing up and what I thought I wanted out of life.

"Here we are," Charley said with quiet pride when we descended the dusty, unpaved road and the forested, picture-perfect small mountain lake came into view. "This is Cherry Lake."

We loaded our camping gear into his canoe and paddled to a secluded cove. Together we dragged the boat up onto the shore and scouted for some level ground. We set up a tent and then went for a long swim. High-altitude lakes are usually painfully cold; this one was invitingly warm. Taking long, leisurely strokes and filling my lungs with mountain air, I felt deeply content, happy that Charley had brought us here.

The next morning, we hiked up a steep, rocky stream. It was challenging, but I felt safe in Charley's company. He seemed adventurous but not too far out of my league. As we clambered up the rocks together, I noticed something. *This feels like family.*

On the way home, we stopped at a rustic restaurant in Sonora. Sitting across from Charley, waiting for our dinner in the pine-paneled, warmly lit dining room, I looked at him and thought, *I think I could marry this guy.* Later, Charley would tell me that he was sitting across from me thinking, *She's magnificent; too bad she's impossible.*

A few months later, we were hurrying home from work to one another's embrace. When Charley suggested that we start a family in two years, we moved in together. However, two years came and went, and we were still not married. Charley was hesitant to commit and reluctant to have a child. I felt a profound sense of betrayal. I was hopelessly torn between a desire to dump him and fear of the ticking biological clock. After what felt like an eternity, Charley proposed. We married, and by the time I was thirty-seven, we had two babies.

By his choice, Charley was working six days a week and attending frequent evening meetings. When he finally got home at 10:00 or 10:30, he would give me a warm kiss, ask about my day, eat some leftover dinner, and then head back to his study. Although I, too, was working, my life with young children was very different. A picture in our photo album captures the deliciously earthy, tactile, and utterly overwhelming chaos of this period. I am breastfeeding our new infant daughter and also consulting on the phone with a colleague while our two-year-old son curiously examines the other breast protruding from my nursing bra's still-open flap. Charley's busyness enabled him to remain on the fringes of this overwhelm. I had no such option.

My resentment increased during our children's preschool years. "It's not fair that it should always be *my* ass in the wringer if one of the kids is sick or our childcare falls through," I blasted Charley one day. "Why is it always *my* problem, *my* frantic search, or *my* clients who get jerked around if I can't find someone to care for them?" But Charley flatly refused to take a turn at staying home, citing that his full-time work brought us more income than mine. His explanation made me gasp with feminist horror.

I was angry. But under the anger and resentment, I felt ashamed. My husband's work seemed more meaningful to him than our family and more important than our marriage. However, the most enduring hurt was something else. Both of us knew that Charley had seen me floundering and had chosen to look away.

Things finally came to a head when Shahla and Mischa were four and six. Charley casually mentioned a series of Tuesday night meetings coming up. Tuesdays were the only weekday evening Charley reliably got home in time for all of us to have dinner together. I gave him an ultimatum. "Take six months to think this over, but if you still aren't willing to give more of yourself to our family, I really don't want to be married to you." Charley has never taken kindly to coercion, and his reply was shockingly blunt: "Well, I'd miss you. You've been a good wife."

Six months went by. Nothing changed. I didn't leave.

Looking back, I can see that we were trying, unsuccessfully, to reconcile our different visions of being a family. Here were two smart people in a hopeless standoff over sharing the tasks of caregiving, homemaking, and providing financially. Charley's total immersion in work was preemptive and unilateral. My ultimatum was provocative and unproductive. We had yet to learn how to negotiate his dreams and mine.

After enduring many power struggles, we eventually came up with a creative idea: an annual planning retreat. Here is what prompted it. One evening, Charley informed me that in addition to his customary six-day workweek, he would be gone all day Sunday attending a strategic planning retreat for his professional organization. My anger was immediate and intense. I shot back: "How about a planning retreat for *this* organization: your family!"

"Good idea," said Charley.

———

And indeed, it was a good idea. At home, we tend to get so busy with daily life that we end up talking about everything *except* what is most important. Our retreats give us a weekend away every year to think deeply about our lives and our marriage.

Over the past twenty years, we've evolved a process that feels intimate, romantic even, and lets us deal efficiently with a wide range of topics. If we have been waiting for a safe setting and some uninterrupted time to bring up a relationship issue, a heartfelt dream, a household matter, or an especially sensitive subject, this is it.

To start each retreat on a positive note, Charley and I begin with a tender warm-up ritual. We each write down "ten things I love about you" and then read our lists to each other. Initially, it was much easier to think of "ten things that aggravate me about you." But now I look forward to telling Charley what I love about him. I always mention his buff fitness; he always includes my splendid smile.

My favorite retreat exercise is the "Satisfaction Scale."[1] Charley and I separately rate our current satisfaction with important aspects of our lives: family, love, home, friends, health, money, work, community. We learn a lot by comparing our lists. Satisfaction with *love* tends to be similar; satisfaction with *home*, not so much. When our ratings on a given item are very discrepant, we know we have a good discussion topic for the weekend.

Over the years, we have used our retreats to make some important decisions: whether to move to a nearby community (we did); whether to have a third baby (we didn't); and whether Charley will ever retire (unlikely). We always discuss how our children are doing and what needs they may have now or in the future. We've also used our time to plan vacations and important celebrations.

Our planning and problem-solving usually go smoothly, but sometimes we get triggered. Feelings of closeness and collaboration can vanish in a flash, and when they do, we revert to our hopelessly frustrated, argumentative former selves. That's when we know to call a halt. We need time by ourselves to do something calming and pleasurable. I usually listen to music; Charley takes a walk. We return at an agreed-upon time and move to an easier topic. Later, we'll revisit the one that burst into flames.

Recreation is part of every retreat. Charley and I make time each day for a hike, a bike ride, or a swim, and perhaps some good loving followed by a nap. A hefty dose of physical exercise brings us back to our task refreshed.

It is a relief to be able to deal calmly with subjects that would raise hackles at home. We have successfully broached some very sensitive topics and resolved them. We've confronted responsible

---

1. See the appendix for a version of this Satisfaction Scale for your own use, as well as other retreat materials and instructions.

tracking of money, personal hygiene, end-of-life planning, and—a topic almost worse than death—the need for hearing aids.

Our agendas are always full. In two decades, Charley and I have never run out of material.

—

When we eventually honed our problem-solving and negotiating skills, I no longer got into household-related arguments with Charley. Instead, I began to tease him. "Look, Charley, you do whatever you think is fair. But keep in mind, if I'm ever on the *Oprah Winfrey Show*, I plan to tell it like it is."

To my astonishment, several years later, a producer from the *Oprah Winfrey Show* called. They were preparing an episode called "Is Your Marriage Equal?" and invited me to be their guest expert. They must have learned about my work with couples because I was an occasional media expert on the impact of work/family stress on marriage.

When Charley came home that night, I greeted him gleefully. "Guess who called today?" After I told him my news, Charley calmly reached into his wallet and handed me a piece of paper. It was a typed list titled "All the Things I Do for You, Our Children, and Our Home."

I gave Charley an incredulous, quizzical look. Smiling, he said, "I wasn't taking any chances, just in case Oprah ever *did* call!"

"Well, Charley," I said, laughing with appreciation, "I guess you really *do* believe in me."

—

I was shaking with anxiety on the flight to Chicago, in the hotel, and at the studio the following morning. Anxiety? Not exactly; how about gut terror?

On the dais were five couples. Some of the wives were wage earners; others were home full time. Some of the fathers participated at home; others did not. Some couples liked their arrangement; for others, one spouse was satisfied and the other discontent. Oprah asked which ones I thought had an equal marriage.

"I believe couples have an equal marriage when both partners are satisfied with *whatever* arrangement they work out."

The discrepancy between Charley's satisfaction with our arrangement and mine was at the heart of our conflict. Charley was comfortable with a very traditional division of labor. I most definitely was not. The more Charley left me out of decisions that impacted my life, the angrier and more disparaging I became. Angry enough that I sometimes wondered if I'd married the wrong guy.

Our retreats helped us look honestly at our marriage and become skillful at making shared decisions about our future. Although the retreat process was born out of frustration and fury, we used it to extricate ourselves from a long, painful stalemate. Charley and I grew to trust the process and, more importantly, to trust each other.

———

Ten days after our arrival in Ecuador, the Pachamama journey concludes with a fitting ceremony and loving farewells. It is surprising how close our group has grown in such a short time. Well, maybe not so surprising. We have trekked through the jungle together; we have taken hallucinogens together; we have been naked together. No wonder we feel close! But now, Charley and I will travel on our own for a week.

As the end of the vacation comes into view without any further discussion of traveling for an extended time, I grow worried. "Charley, are we ever going to have that conversation you agreed to?"

"I haven't forgotten about it. I just want to wait until we get to the coast."

"Well, it's our last chance before we go home."

Earlier in our marriage, I felt controlled by Charley's need to determine the timing of conversations. But I've come to understand. Since I am the one who initiates most of the changes in our lives—buying a house, having children, or moving to a different community—one of the ways Charley manages these changes is by determining the timing of discussions. It's killing me to wait, but I know that anything else will backfire.

———

As we approach the coast, we see tankers offshore and notice petroleum pipelines parallel to the highway. The sand at the beach is brown with occasional black oily patches. Our lodging is filled with cobwebs and spiders and the aroma of mildew. Is *this* what we drove across Ecuador to enjoy? We decide to make the best of it, and in the morning, we wander along the sand to a cleaner part of the beach. Hot and thirsty, we find an inviting outdoor restaurant where we sit down and order a huge pitcher of freshly made lemonade. We gulp down the first glass, thirstily drink the second, and by the third glass, we are finally capable of sipping the tart and refreshing drink.

"Now," says Charley, "would be a good time to have that talk."

Finally, I think. *Well, here goes.* "Charley," I begin. "If I'm ever going to have a chance to travel and spend time in other cultures, it had better happen soon. Given my spine issues, the days of sleeping on funky beds are numbered. I would so love for us to take a year off from work and travel together. Would you be willing to take a sabbatical with me? Please?"

I know perfectly well what his answer will be.

"No. I want to keep working," Charley replies without any hesitation.

I sit there thinking. Not thinking exactly; more like making space for a thought to come.

"Well then," I counter. "What if you were to keep working and I go traveling?"

Charley's response is swift and emphatic. "Well, I would *hate* to be without you for a year!" These words are delivered in what I call his "case is closed" voice. I feel myself tighten up. In years past, I would have jumped right in with arguments or debate. Now, I wait.

After a significant pause, he quietly amends his remark. "But I *would* like to support your dreams."

"Good. I can live with that," I say flippantly. Behind the flippancy lies the hard work of a marriage-transforming commitment. Several years ago, at one of our planning retreats, we agreed that important issues would not be settled until each of us was able to say, "I can live with that." Our ultimate decision didn't necessarily have to make us both happy; sometimes that just wasn't possible. But it would need to be acceptable to each of us and mutually agreed upon. Over the years, this commitment has served us well, providing an important sense of safety.

We've been talking around this subject of travel for several years, but I've never made a specific proposal. Even though this isn't a formal retreat, my understanding of the negotiating process is foremost in my mind as we embark on this momentous conversation. I'm sure that is true for Charley as well.

———

Over lunch, I ask Charley, "If I really were to be away for a year, what would be the hardest part for you?" I know perfectly well what his response will be.

"No sex."

I don't say anything, but I'm thinking, *Of course.* Of course, months of sexual abstinence would be a major obstacle for

Charley. Earlier in our lives, a lengthy separation like the one we are starting to discuss would have been out of the question. Even now, in our sixties, it poses a challenge for both of us.

"Hey, honey. I'll need to come back every three or four months to check on my mother and see you and the kids. And if you visited me a couple of times during the year, we could be together every six weeks or so."

"Six weeks is still a long time to go without sex."

"I agree that it's a long time to wait. It will be a long wait for me too. However, while you're at home, I'll be busy having the adventures of a lifetime, so I'll be content to wait. But perhaps we can keep this as an open question with you. I'd never want us to do anything that would threaten our marriage, and I know you feel the same way. But here's what *I* think," I say confidently—perhaps too confidently. "It's possible that a brief encounter with someone else—if it *absolutely* did not lead to an ongoing relationship—might be something I could handle."

Charley looks at me with astonishment.

"If it becomes something you want, we should talk about it. For me, the important part is being totally up front with each other. That's what I consider being faithful in a marriage."

There is no doubt that I have Charley's complete attention.

"The main problem for me," I continue, "is that I don't see how you can be absolutely certain you wouldn't get involved."

"No problem," he says.

"How can you be so sure? Sometimes it's hard for you to know what you're feeling."

"I'm sure. For one thing, it would only happen out of town. And I would be completely up front about our situation, so there would be no confusion."

We pause while he orders more lemonade. As soon as the waiter leaves, Charley looks at me warmly and says, "I probably wouldn't do anything at all, but the sense of freedom would be great."

For a moment I think the issue is settled. But then he says, "There's one problem here. I wouldn't be comfortable if *you* had sex with someone else while we're apart. I know it's not fair, but that's how I feel."

His admission does not surprise me. "Look, Charley, it doesn't make sense to act like we're the same, because we aren't. If I were to have sex with someone else, it would be because I *wanted* to get involved."

The more Charley and I talk seriously about my proposal, the more I realize how much I want this grown-up gap year. Until this very moment, I've never really believed it could happen. I fervently want Charley to say yes, and amazingly, it seems like he might. Imagine! A year of unencumbered time for traveling and exploring. It would be like reaching into the past, making happier choices, and getting to live an experience long since written off as a squandered opportunity.

I can hardly breathe. If Charley is willing to say yes, I will joyfully reciprocate in any way I can. I sincerely doubt that my obsessively hardworking husband will take me up on my offer. But even if he does have a brief encounter while I am away, I truly believe we'll be OK. Despite being unsure of myself in so many other ways, I've always felt confident and assured as a sexual partner. Charley is lucky to have me.

Our conversation at the ocean culminates with Charley saying that with my attention to his main concerns, he is happy to give his blessing.

Everything ceases for a moment while his words sink in. And suddenly I am shivering with excitement and disbelief. I've been nurturing this dream, almost unaware, for my whole adult life. And now, it is *really* going to happen! I look at Charley with a full heart and a huge smile and ask, "Will you please say it one more time?"

He grins back, happy to oblige. "Given what we've discussed, I'm OK with your going traveling for a year."

CHAPTER 5

Preparing to Leap

CALIFORNIA

I am stopped at a red light. It is October, a month before I am to leave on my solo sabbatical. I'm heading to the pharmacy to arrange a four-month supply of prescription medications. This should cover the first portion of my sabbatical. However, I will not be going to Casa Mojanda. It turned out I wasn't eligible for their internship because it required fluency in Spanish. Instead, I've chosen to start my journey in Costa Rica, a notoriously friendly country with excellent Spanish language schools.

To my left, in a sporty black convertible, is a group of blond girls in their late teens or early twenties, loud music pouring from their car radio. It's a sunny fall afternoon and I am filled with happy anticipation of my upcoming journey. In my staid silver Honda, I'm cheerfully shoulder-dancing to the beat of their music. I glance over and notice the attractive young women watching and smiling. I overhear one girl say to the others, "Isn't that cute!"

Now, the only thing that makes my rocking out to the music "cute" is the fact of my gray hair and wrinkles. I wonder where young people get the idea that there is a statute of limitations on rhythm, joy, or moments of abandon.

My impending sabbatical has attracted surprise, curiosity, and admiration from people in all areas of my life. If I were twenty-two instead of sixty-one, a year devoted to solo travel, exploration, language study, and volunteer work would be relatively unexceptional. At my age and given my marital status, I seem to be rocking the boat.

Although my dream of open-ended travel was conceived in my early twenties, preparing for an extended journey involves very different tasks for a woman in her sixties. In my twenties, I'd have had fewer responsibilities but more concerns about money. I could have departed more spontaneously but would have struggled with the challenge of leaving friends and perhaps a boyfriend. At this stage of life, my challenges include the lengthy process of closing a therapy practice after thirty-two years and making care arrangements for my elderly mother. Hence, my preparation begins more than a year before I pack my bags and kiss my husband goodbye at the airport.

———

Closing a therapy practice is never done lightly. Deep attachments form between clients and therapists, and they go in both directions. Typically, therapists go away for no more than a few weeks of vacation each year. I personally don't know anyone who has closed a private psychotherapy practice to take a lengthy sabbatical. I know a few clinicians who have moved away. I know about retirement. And sadly, my colleagues and I know far too much about careers that have ended abruptly due to terminal illnesses.

I am amazed by how serene and unambivalent I have felt throughout the entire process of letting go, from informing my clients eight months in advance, to their poignant goodbyes, to finding another therapist to sublet my office, to packing up books and handing over my keys. I keep waiting to freak out, waiting to have my predictably intense fear reaction of "Oh my God, what have I done?" I brace for my characteristic anxiety and doubt. I wait . . . and wait. It never comes. Instead, I continue to feel grateful and excited. *Where has the old Leah gone, and who is this joyful person who has taken over her body?* I wonder if it's possible that during that arduous night on ayahuasca, I really *did* purge something I no longer needed.

In the final months of therapy, as my clients and I prepare to say goodbye, our therapeutic work intensifies. Themes of adventure and pursuing dreams emerge. A successful working mom who was raised in a competitive family of females acknowledges her feelings of envy. "I feel a little jealous of you identifying and going after your dream," she says. "Travel is not mine, but it makes me want to make each part of my life—my job, my marriage, and my homelife—more like a dream come true."

These therapy endings, coming all at the same time, combine to give me unaccustomed feedback about the meanings and value of therapy to clients. The most surprising feedback about my chosen career comes from a woman as she reflects on mothering her two young daughters. She has worked long and hard in therapy to become different from her own mother, to grow up emotionally and break a cycle of raising children who feel obliged to protect and parent their own parents. "Because of our work together, I can feel good about what I have to give, and I don't need to feel so ashamed about what I don't have," she tells me. "You've helped me become the mother I wanted to be." Crying now, she continues, "I look at my daughters, and I realize that children who aren't even born yet will have better lives because of what we did together."

Whew! Somehow, I'd never let myself take more than fleeting credit for my part in the growth of my clients. This feedback helps me close my practice after three decades with appreciation for my own professional and personal growth.

———

There is another major task I need to address before my sabbatical can begin. In addition to winding down my clinical practice, I need to arrange appropriate care for my mother. At the age of ninety-one, she has been a widow for four years and is in the middle stage of dementia. Despite these challenges, Mother still lives in her own home, defensively insisting that she has *always* been absent-minded and needs no help, thank you very much. Any discussion of assisted living ends in uproar.

Overwhelmed, we reach out to an eldercare consultant who introduces us to the *therapeutic lie*. "At this stage, it is far more respectful to go behind the elder's back and arrange what she needs than to explain why it is necessary and seek her consent. The therapeutic lie is far kinder than the truth because it allows her to maintain some dignity."

So, on my next visit to the desert, I get copies of the existing legal documents giving me power of attorney for my mother. I also obtain a letter from her physician stating that my mother is no longer able to care for herself. I consolidate her funds in a single bank and begin setting up automatic payments for her most important bills.

As I carry out my duties as power of attorney, I feel like a caring daughter. I also feel like a deceptive person, engaging in forbidden behavior. My actions feel like a betrayal of the straight-forward, authentic relationships I believe in. Nevertheless, I see how they avert the stubborn rants and meltdowns that have been part of nearly every recent trip. But under all the disheveled white hair, the confusion and forgetting, she is still my mother, and I know I am *not* supposed to lie to her.

A representative at the organization managing her retire-ment fund informs me that Mother herself must sign their in-house power of attorney form. When I protest, the woman on the phone informs me, sotto voce, that no one is likely to notice if I just forge her signature. While I have gradually grown able to tolerate looking my mother in the eye and telling a therapeutic lie, the "therapeutic felony" remains out of reach for me.

Even as I make arrangements for my mom, I struggle with conflicting feelings. This is my mother in decline. How dare I leave her for months on end?

I am not sure my mother has made the connection that my travels will change my pattern of flying to Arizona every month for three days. Just once, she asks, "You'll be traveling for a whole year?" I assure her that I'll be back to see her every three to four months. "I'll be traveling on the quarter system, just like I did in college," I explain. "But I won't come see you every month as I have been."

"You don't come every month; no way!" Mother insists.

Perhaps she can only remember the rhythm of years past, before my father's death and before her dementia, when I came to visit once or twice a year.

"How often do you think I come to see you?" I ask.

"I don't know exactly. Often, but *not* every month."

"*Often* sounds right. Let's agree on *often*," I say, and the squalls on the emotional sea subside.

Given my mother's early life, it is small wonder that separations make her anxious. One traumatic loss followed another during her childhood. Her mother died giving birth to her. Her father had a fatal heart attack when she was two and a half. Taken in by her aunt, my mother and her older sister became part of a large, lively family where she lived until age five. Then, as my mother put it, she was "given away"—adopted by distant relatives, an elderly childless couple that she'd never met. Over time, she grew deeply attached to her adoptive father, a sensitive and loving man. To her horror, he died unexpectedly when she was eleven. Charley used to say with admiration that given this history of loss, the fact my mother got out of bed each morning and put her feet on the floor was an act of true heroism.

Her long and happy marriage to my dad was a profound source of security and stability for her. Yet her anxiety about separation never left her. Losing her husband was devastating. She never stopped grieving, but she bravely soldiered on.

Mother's fear that separation can be dangerous to the one who leaves or the one who is left—that indeed it can be fatal—was unspoken. Yet it somehow found its way inside *my* body, where it coexists along with an inquisitive and outgoing spirit.

I am *ready* for this adventure. It's not like when I left home to go to college in California and promptly developed my lifelong fear of dying in an earthquake. My father's death helped me understand that dying is not a risk; it's a certainty. Life is finite, and at a certain point, consigning important dreams to "someday" no longer makes sense. Although the timing of my sabbatical is not ideal in terms of my mom, our mother-daughter bond is secure. And for the time being, her care situation is secure as well. The final piece falls into place when my brother offers to come in autumn and stay with our mother while I travel. I am *so* relieved and grateful. A long visit from her son is an arrangement my mother can accept while maintaining her dignity.

After my return to California, my mother sends me a note: "I rejoice in your well-deserved sabbatical from a fine career." She is happy for me that I'm about to have a travel adventure. I am touched by her generosity of spirit. As attuned as my mother is to separation, she *has* to realize that my travels mean separation. Even though she can no longer track the passage of time, in blessing my journey, she is offering me a precious gift.

My partially packed suitcase has been sprawled on the bedroom floor for three months. Charley is amazingly tolerant of the clutter. I am determined to take only a carry-on bag and a small backpack. The clothing part is easy; the challenging parts are my snorkel gear, camera, toiletries, prescription medications, and shoe orthotics. These things take up room and add weight. But what if I need them . . . ?

How brilliant we humans are at creating distractions to manage our anxiety before a big transition. As I prepare to leave for my sabbatical, I become obsessed with travel luggage. I am looking for a lightweight rolling carry-on, a comfortable small women's pack, and a well-designed travel purse. Rationally, I know that the success of my journey will not be a function of my luggage, but I can't help myself. Invariably, I find that none is lighter or holds more than my tattered, fifteen-year-old rolling fabric suitcase.

While I decide what to pack and what to jettison and while I wait for the rainy season to subside in Costa Rica, word of my sabbatical has gotten around. In addition to curiosity and admiration, my upcoming journey elicits other kinds of wonder. One friend, bolder than the rest, asks me point-blank, "Is your marriage OK?"

"It's definitely OK," I assure her. "I would never gamble on being away from Charley for a year if it weren't."

"How do your kids feel about your taking a sabbatical?" another friend wants to know.

"They are proud of their mom," I answer with certainty. "Both of them have been to Costa Rica to study Spanish, and they are glad their travels helped blaze a trail for me."

Along with curiosity and respect, envy is another emotion evoked by my travel plans. I've always been sensitive to the envy of others. More than once, somebody tells me, "I am so jealous!" At first, I don't know how to respond. Then I remember: envy is how I know there's something important I want for myself. Now I reply, "It sounds like you've got some dreams of your own. You'd better figure out what they are and make them happen."

Despite my discomfort with others' envy, I can't help but laugh when one of my favorite male colleagues says, "Tell your husband I'll marry him in a minute. I'd sure like someone to sponsor *me* for a year of travel." It's funny, but inside, I bristle a little. My goal is to sponsor myself. It's true that Charley has offered his help if I need it. But I intend to travel frugally: I have savings from my therapy practice, frequent-flier miles will cover my airfare, and homestays in each country will let me live inexpensively and meet local people.

———

My sabbatical is finally about to begin. I am leaving for Costa Rica in the morning. My plan is to progress from easier to more challenging destinations, and I've been told Costa Rica would be a friendly place to start.

I *must* be ready to go because I've been crabby with Charley. Everything about him bugs me. It takes a while for me to understand what's going on: I think I've been trying to render Charley unimportant so it won't be so hard to leave him. I confess this to my husband and wonder what I can do to overcome it. Charley promptly replies, "Why don't you try saying, 'Charley, you stud muffin, ravish me!'"

Laughing, I let myself face the obvious: Life is fragile and finite. Something could happen to me . . . or to him. In the game of tag, when you let go of home base, you are no longer safe. In the game of Life, home base only provides the illusion of safety. But it is a comforting illusion. This solo journey definitely feels like letting go of home base.

I had a disturbing dream a couple of weeks before my departure. In the dream, I look down at my hand and discover that my wedding band is broken. Instead of being a fully enclosed circle of metal, the ring has opened up. The dream nags at me for days. Could I have secret plans for myself that will blow my life apart? The thought is frightening. When I describe my dream to a close friend, she listens carefully and then offers her wisdom: "I think it means that you are breaking the confines of conventional marriage. You and Charley are making more space in your marriage to allow you to pursue your dreams."

I feel relief. My friend is right. Charley and I are loosening the marital ties, not out of indifference, but out of acceptance that we are separate people with separate dreams.

Throughout my sabbatical, I will meet budget travelers of all ages. Many will have quit their jobs in order to travel, which means they'll face the uncertainty of finding new employment when they return home. Some will have rented out their houses or sublet their apartments. They will stay in hostels or homes or campgrounds. They will travel on public buses. While their financial circumstances may differ greatly, these adventure travelers have one thing in common. *They have dared to let go.* Each of them has relinquished the safe and familiar to make space for the new and unexpected. After so many years of yearning to join the ranks of these explorers—free spirits who set off without an itinerary, a timetable, or reservations—I feel amazed and elated that I've finally gained the confidence and found the courage to be one of them.

———

The evening before my departure turns into an all-nighter. I haul my suitcase and the huge pile of stuff I've now accumulated across the hall into our son's old bedroom. Through the night while Charley sleeps, I pack and repack. There is simply no way I can take everything I want and still be able to carry it comfortably. In the end, I reluctantly jettison my snorkel and fins, a new camera, and some clothing. I take out half of my medications; Charley can bring the other half when he visits me. I insist on making space for my "kid kit." As a way to interact with children along the way, I'm taking art supplies, an inflatable globe, a puppet, tiny dinosaurs, and other plastic animals. It is 5:00 a.m. before everything is stuffed into my suitcase and small pack.

I finally crawl into bed at 5:12. It feels *so* good. Charley holds me passionately and whispers, "The alarm is going to go off in three minutes." When it does, I hit the snooze button, and we snuggle fiercely against one another. Pressed against Charley's warm body, I wonder, *Why am I leaving this comfortable bed, this perfect climate, and these sweet embraces for a place I know will be miserably hot and humid, where I'll be alone and probably have to sleep on some lumpy bed?* But it's too late to ponder such questions. It's time to go to the airport.

CHAPTER 6

Falling in Love

COSTA RICA

The moment the plane doors open, warm, tropical air envelops me. It's 9:00 p.m. in Liberia, Costa Rica. I clear customs and exit the small airport pulling my rolling carry-on and wearing my backpack. Looking around for a taxi, I notice among the waiting drivers a man with my name on a sign. Apparently, the school has arranged for a driver to meet me. I approach him. "*Soy la Señora Fisher.*" My language tapes are already proving helpful. Soon we are on our way to Playa Samara, the Pacific beach town where I will live and study Spanish for the next six weeks.

I attempt to converse with the driver, Elio, although each time I think of something to say, I realize there is a crucial word I don't know. Still, I do my best. We listen to radio music. Exhausted from my all-nighter, I doze, wake up, and doze again. Elio tells me with sweet encouragement that I have many words: "*Usted tiene muchas, muchas palabras.*" Elio's acknowledgment is amusing in its accuracy. I can't exactly *speak* Spanish yet, but apparently, I have a good collection of words. I can only imagine how resounding the silence of this ride must be for students who arrive in Costa Rica with no *palabras* at all.

It grows foggy and cooler as we near the Pacific Coast beaches. The terrain has become hilly, and even in the dark, I can see there are more trees. The simple stucco houses are somewhat bigger as we approach the coast. And then we are in Samara. Elio pulls into the driveway of an attractive stucco house with three white sofas on the spacious front veranda.

My hosts, Claudia and Fernando, come out. The woman is middle-aged; her husband appears to be considerably older. In response to my "*Buenas noches*," Claudia comes over and gives me a hug. She takes my arm and snugs it firmly under hers, steers me around the house, and shows me to my room. Judging from its location at the back of the driveway, it must have once been a garage. Claudia chatters all the while in Spanish I can't comprehend. I may not understand her explanations, but the physical warmth of her body puts me at ease. Although this is *my* first homestay, Claudia has had fleets of students. She explains that her family owns a restaurant, and I will go there for all my meals. I am relieved. This means I can order what I want and be spared any pressure to overeat out of politeness to my host. The room that will be mine has a bathroom and its own entrance. There are two beds: a double and a single. I can sleep in one and store all my stuff on the other. There is a small nightstand, a standing fan, and a piece of driftwood in the corner. That is all, and it is enough. Claudia hands me the key, and I learn a new word: *clave*. I gratefully thank my hosts, turn on the fan, and fall into bed.

———

The next morning, I wake after a sound sleep, despite the foam mattress being even worse than I had feared. In fact, it has been so thoroughly slept on that there's a permanent indentation in the middle. It slopes from five inches of foam on the perimeter to barely an inch in the center. I dread the thought of sleeping for weeks on what is essentially a wooden board. But I guess this is part of the adventure.

I dress and go outside. Surprisingly, it is already hot and humid. Birdsong fills the air. A woman appears and introduces herself as Blanca. She is Claudia and Fernando's adult daughter, and she will take me around the block to the family's restaurant. As we're nearing the restaurant, I hear a startling warble. I look up to see the bird and stumble over a crumbling, uneven slab of sidewalk. I pick myself up quickly, but my ankle is turned, and my knee is bleeding. *No hay problema.* Blanca takes me to a *farmacia* directly across the street from their restaurant. Soon I have an ACE bandage for my ankle and a Band-Aid for my knee.

After breakfast, I walk the two blocks to the beach. As I face the ocean, I see some young *ticos* (as Costa Ricans are called) playing volleyball directly in front of me. Down the beach to the left, I can see the surfing area. Turning right, I walk along the sand past a couple of outdoor cafés until I reach the large sign: INTERCULTURA. An arrow points toward a two-story, yellow stucco building. This is my school. I enter the air-conditioned office, where a receptionist greets me and hands me a registration packet.

I return to my room, put on a bathing suit and sarong, and then head back to the beach for my first swim. Thanks to an offshore reef, the waves are gentle in the curve of the bay where my school is located. The ocean is a blissful, perfect temperature. I am by myself, and I am happy. After my long flight the day before, swimming in the ocean feels glorious.

As I emerge from the water, I notice a group of people clustered around a spot high on the beach near a line of palm trees. I walk toward them and discover they are excitedly watching turtle babies hatching. "I have never, *ever* seen turtles lay their eggs on this beach before," says a friendly American who I'll find out is the surfing instructor.

"This country certainly knows how to entertain its visitors," I tell him.

The little hatchlings are about three inches long. They emerge from eggs buried in the sand and climb over one another as they dig their way up to the surface. From here, they will face a steep learning curve as they make their way across the hot sand to the water a mere two hundred feet away. Babies of all species are adorable, and we watch in fascination as these tiny *tortugas* begin their journey to the sea. They awkwardly splay their four little flippers, butts wagging like puppies' tails. By the time they approach the water, some have died from the effort and the heat; the rest have become coordinated and efficient little marchers. People gather spontaneously to watch and protect them, shooing away curious dogs or lifting some of the miniature creatures and carrying them to the water. I am witnessing survival of the fittest—with a little human intervention. "Most baby sea turtles," explains somebody near me, "will shortly become lunch for some marine predator. Only two out of every hundred will survive." I know that Costa Rica is protective of its wildlife, but I never imagined I'd encounter *tortugas* on my very first morning in Costa Rica. Although I don't know any of the people around me, we form an instant community as we welcome and escort these tiny creatures to the sea. I hope my own launch will be as successful.

———

I spend the rest of my first day walking around Playa Samara, beaming with happiness. I smile and say, "*Hola*," and people are genuinely responsive, cheerful, and kind. In a little notebook, I begin writing down the names of the people I meet so I won't forget. Elio is the taxi driver. Soon I will add others: Ricardo, a.k.a. Tío Tigre, rents boogie boards and lives across the street from my host family with his wife and their newborn baby. Lucia is the Canadian woman who works at the internet café across the road from my family's restaurant. Mariana, Elisa, and Daniel are the employees in the restaurant.

When I return after dark to my room at the end of the driveway, I realize that I have not been scared one little bit! My conclusions so far about Samara: the natives are friendly, the sidewalks not so much. As I prepare for bed, I change the bandage on my knee and remember how I used to tell my kids, "If you don't get at least one owie every day, you haven't had enough fun." Well, I can honestly say at the end of the first day of my sabbatical that I've had a great deal of fun.

———

Shortly after my arrival in Costa Rica, I have a nightmare. Before going to bed, I wash some underwear and set the old fan in my room on rotate so that I can simultaneously dry my laundry and keep cool as I sleep. I drape my wet clothing over the piece of driftwood in the corner of the room. Toward morning, I dream that Charley has knowingly lied to me about our financial situation. He told me we were in good shape for my sabbatical, but in fact, we are in dire financial circumstances, and now I've given up my livelihood. This is a marital deal-breaker, and there's no choice but to divorce him. In my dream, I know I must leave him, but I dread it, fearing that I will dive into a deep depression.

Finally, I drag myself out of sleep to find that I'm drenched in sweat. The fan has gotten stuck during the night. So much for multitasking: my laundry is still wet, and I am plastered to the sheets and dehydrated. During the night, my physical discomfort has produced a dream about a miserably uncomfortable choice. Either I can have this glorious adventure, or I can have my marriage, but not both. It doesn't take long to figure out this is a dream about separation guilt. My success in traveling solo and my delight at being in Costa Rica must have triggered fear that I am somehow harming my marriage. Wiping my face with cool water, I remind myself that because of the goodwill Charley and I have cultivated over three decades, and because of our thoughtful planning, I *can* have my cake and eat it too, at least for this period of time. I don't have to get a divorce. I only have to get some water and email Charley that I have safely arrived.

The following day, I spend three hours at the internet café composing a long group letter to Charley and the people who have asked to be my sabbatical pen pals. Kind Lucia from Quebec, who came to study Spanish and stayed, advises me to save my document every few minutes. "Not only are these computers incredibly slow," she explains, "but on an overcast day like this one, the rain can knock out the power." A clap of thunder punctuates her advice, its intensity making me jump.

When I complete my letter home, announcing my safe arrival and glorious first days in Costa Rica, the computer rejects my efforts when I hit "send." "Too many recipients," says Lucia when she sees how many names are on my sabbatical pen pal list. She instructs me to divide the eighty-four addresses into four lists.

Lucia comments that eighty-four is a lot of friends. I reply dismissively that when you live in one place for forty years, the list adds up. "That is a lot of friends," she reiterates. Afterward, walking home to my host family's house in the rain, carefully avoiding the potholes and puddles, I take in the truth of what Lucia has said. Eighty-four people who want to follow me on this journey, who wish me well as I leave the security of my marriage and my comfort zone. How surprising to be supposedly on my own and simultaneously encircled by friends.

———

Within a very few days, I settle into a routine. My morning begins with the utterly predictable pleasure of breakfast at my *tico* family's restaurant, an open-air affair on the main street of town. I always order the same thing: café negro, scrambled eggs, and a plate of tropical fruit. The coffee is rich and strong. The fruit plate consists of a banana sliced lengthwise, circles of ripe papaya, triangles of pineapple, and either watermelon triangles or orange slices. They look like what we eat at home, but they sing with sweetness and flavor. My mindfulness practice for the day is simply to focus my attention on the joyful pleasure of tasting each piece of fruit. I especially enjoy the peaceful moments before the first fly wanders by, discovers my breakfast, and signals to all his fly friends in the neighborhood. How *do* they do that?

Walking along the beach to school on my first day of classes, I find horses wandering freely in the shallow water. I am dazzled by the almost magical scene. When I reach the school, I push open the wooden gate and step from the sand to a fenced-in grassy yard. I've entered a beautiful little sanctuary where I will find warmhearted people, air-conditioned classrooms, and playful purpose.

Ulysses, one of the staff members, greets me by name: "*Buenos días, Señora Leah.*" I met him on my first day in Samara. Now he is high on a scaffold, touching up the colorfully painted sea creatures that adorn the school's yellow two-story building. On the lawn, students from all over the world are getting acquainted. The bell rings, and we move inside. Even at eight o'clock in the morning, I am grateful for the air-conditioning. I find my classroom and take a seat at the square table. Although the room is small, large windows offer a spectacular view of the ocean. By the time the bell rings, there are six of us: a young man of twenty, two middle-aged couples, and me. I am the oldest, but not by as much as I had expected. Our teacher is Melvin (pronounced "Melbin"), a tall dark-haired man in his late twenties.

To get us speaking Spanish right from the start and to cut through typically boring introductions, Melvin instructs us to introduce our eight-year-old selves. The teachers must only speak Spanish in class, so to help us understand, Melvin accompanies his conversation with elaborate pantomimes that are both brilliant and hilarious. As soon as I have enough vocabulary, I will tease him that I must have enrolled in Teatro Intercultura rather than Escuela Intercultura.

The school's openness to playful teaching and learning becomes evident the day we practice the past tense. On the board, Melvin writes a long Spanish name: José Figueres Ferrer. He then invites us to invent a biography for this *hombre*. We can make it as wild and crazy as we wish, he instructs. The six of us pull out our dictionaries and get in a huddle. We decide that this *hombre* was born in 1823 and, his name notwithstanding, he was Norwegian. Professionally, he was a pirate. He played the guitar despite the hook that replaced a hand. During his long career, he captured and despoiled many women, resulting in many, many children. To his consternation, he fathered thirty-three daughters and one son. After we've completed the delivery of our class *biografía*, Melvin tells us that José Figueres Ferrer was Costa Rica's beloved three-term president. He was elected in 1949 and 1953 and again in 1970. This forward-thinking leader was responsible for abolishing Costa Rica's army and giving women the vote. For me, learning has never, *ever* been this much fun.

After class, I have lunch at the family's restaurant. Watching tourists at nearby tables engrossed in their guidebooks, I am so glad to be settling into the life of this tiny town rather than visiting every tourist attraction in Costa Rica. Afterward, I stroll along the *calle principal*, Samara's main street, peering into the colorful open-air stalls. One of them sells hammocks, and I choose a vivid purple one. Around the corner is a hardware store, and thanks to my little dictionary, I succeed in buying two generous lengths of rope. Now I can do my homework on the beach from the comfort of my own hammock. After class the following day, I carefully hang my hammock between two palm trees in front of the school and climb in with my workbook and dictionary. I am feeling peaceful and productive as I start my homework. A short while later, a little ice cream truck makes its musical way along the beach. The driver stops in front of me and says something in rapid Spanish. He repeats himself, but I still can't understand. Ultimately, he resorts to Melvin's technique of exaggerated pantomime, and I finally grasp what he's trying to tell me: that I am in imminent danger from the giant coconuts hanging on the trees to which I've fastened my hammock. "*¡Gracias, muchísimas gracias!*" I thank the ice cream man while imagining his opinion of the survival potential of these idiot Norte Americanos. I find two nearby palms that are not laden with coconuts, rehang my hammock, and settle in to memorize vocabulary words.

On the weekend, there is a field trip. Driving to a fiesta in Liberia, I ride shotgun with the school's van driver, Marco. He speaks slowly and clearly, so I use this opportunity to ask questions about marriage in Costa Rica. As a therapist, I've been curious about couple relationships in Costa Rica since before I arrived. I wonder how they are similar and how they differ from our own. I take out my pocket dictionary and look up the words for marriage (*matrimonio*) and for married (*casado* for a man or *casada* for a woman). The word for *married* is distressingly like the word for *tired* (*cansado* or *cansada*). I will have to be careful to keep them straight.

I ask Marco if he is married, and he tells me that he's divorced. I express interest, and he volunteers that he has a six-year-old and a one-year-old. He speaks slowly and patiently, leaving me time to look up words I don't know. As we talk, I gather that it took courage to end his marriage in a culture so dominated by religious condemnation of divorce. His parents were very angry, he tells me.

"How long did they stay angry?" I ask.

"They still are," he replies. "There is more divorce now in Costa Rica, especially in the cities, but it is disapproved of." He continues, "What's much more common is for couples to stay married and be unhappy."

———

I thoroughly enjoy my first two weeks of classes with Melvin and our cohesive little cohort of classmates. We laugh, we play, and we learn Spanish. But now it is Monday again, and my companions have all departed. This week's class consists of one rather humorless couple and me. The transition is hard. Not only do I miss my playful classmates, but the scrape on my knee from that first day has grown infected, and the pharmacist explains that it will never heal if I continue swimming in the ocean. Apparently, the rains bring runoff from the streams, carrying bacteria from the upcountry cattle, chickens, and horses. Without being able to swim and without my *campañeros*, I am lonely. I am also frustrated about being such a slow language learner.

On the beach during a class break one day, Melvin asks me how things are going. To my surprise, I start to cry. In English, I tell him that I am struggling with memorizing vocabulary and all the irregular verb endings. I see how quickly my younger classmates absorb what is being taught. Each day, I study verbs in past, present, and future tense. I study the vocabulary that Melvin writes on the board for us. Yet when I open my mouth in class to say something, the word or the verb ending isn't there. Melvin tells me that I just need to give it time.

Unfortunately, I don't get to practice speaking Spanish with my host family. They leave for the restaurant before I wake up in the mornings, and at night, their car headlights shine in my window as I'm falling asleep. When I applied for this program, my only request was, "Please place me with a really happy family—preferably one with young children." Later, when I meet the homestay coordinator, I ask why he selected this hardworking, unavailable older couple to host me. His answer is revealing.

"When I saw your age, I thought you'd like to have a private bath and separate entrance."

———

My mood dip is so intense that I suspect I'm missing Charley. We have begun to email each other on a daily basis. Compared to our more matter-of-fact conversations at home, our correspondence is charming and romantic. Charley writes his salutations as "Dear Sweetheart" and "*Mi querida esposa.*" I write mine back as "*Hola, mi querido Charley*" and "My darling." We share the events of our day: Charley describes his teaching and visits with our children. I describe my hilarious teacher and the ocean. "Tonight, I swam with pelicans and saw a breathtaking sunset." We notice that it's easier to feel close when we're apart. Our daily emails are like an umbilicus, keeping us securely connected. Later, I'll be struck by how many of my early ones include requests for Charley's help: refilling prescriptions, getting my car smog checked, and interceding with my bank. I will become more adept at taking care of my own needs, but for now, knowing that Charley has my back is reassuring.

———

Although there are words in Spanish for *spring, summer, fall,* and *winter,* Costa Rica only has two seasons: wet season, which is euphemistically called "green season" (*estación verde*) and dry season (*estación seca*). Green season has stretched well into November this year, but when dry season finally arrives, it is dazzling. One day it is humid, hot, rainy, and buggy. The next day it is suddenly sunny and much less humid. There is nothing gradual about this seasonal change. Almost overnight, the huge puddles in Samara dry up, the standing water inside discarded coconuts on the beach dries up, my infected knee is healed, and the mosquitoes are mostly gone. In dry season, this little beach town looks much more attractive. Now it is full of visitors on the weekends, and business is good in my family's restaurant.

After dinner one day, I ask if I can help in the restaurant. Elisa says I can help take orders from the English-speaking customers because sometimes it's difficult to understand them. Now the staff chat with me beyond the requisite *buenos días*.

A few nights later, Mariana puts me to work slipping clean knives and forks into the long, transparent sleeves the restaurant uses for extra cleanliness. Another night, when I poke my head into the kitchen, the cook invites me to cut up vegetables. He hands me a bowl of green beans.

I look in the bowl of long, irregular string beans, and a shiver runs through me. Suddenly I am twenty again, and I've just completed a six-month study abroad program in France. My roommate and I have found au pair positions in a suburb of Paris. What a disappointment I must have been to the mother, a Catholic woman in her thirties, pregnant with her fifth child. I didn't know how to drive, so I couldn't take the children to school. I didn't speak French well enough to shop for groceries, and I was utterly useless in the kitchen.

One Saturday, Madame was getting ready for a dinner party. Between trips to the bathroom to throw up, she asked me to prepare the green beans. The task involved cutting off the ends and removing the strings. There were to be nine of us for dinner. Madame placed a veritable mountain of string beans in front of me. I took the beans one at a time and carefully cut off each end and pulled away the string. I could tell by a glance or two from Madame that there must be a more efficient way, but I didn't know what it was, and I was too embarrassed to ask.

So, what gorgeous symmetry to be holding another enormous bowl of green beans almost forty years later in another foreign country, as I struggle to learn another foreign language. Only this time, the string beans come with a wonderfully sharp chef's knife and enough garnered domestic skills that soon I'm happily and efficiently cutting beans in large clumps. I make short work of the beans, followed by piles of cauliflower and broccoli and carrots. Thinking about those two piles of green beans is a dramatic reminder that despite the late start, I eventually arrived where I wanted to be. I married, had babies, and even figured out how to feed them. Standing in the kitchen of my *tica* family's restaurant, contemplating green beans—past and present—I experience one of those remarkable healing moments.

Three days later, when I come down with a miserable cold and order chicken soup for dinner, I discover the destination for those vegetables. My bowl of salty, flavorful homemade soup is filled with green beans, carrots, cauliflower, and broccoli. I feel comforted in both body and spirit as I sip the steaming soup and study my Spanish verbs.

During the third week, I approach the school administrator and explain that my host family is way too busy to practice Spanish with me and that I'm feeling lonely. She offers to find me a conversation partner. My *compañera de conversación* is Hazel, a charming twenty-two-year-old mother of two who is eager to gain confidence in speaking English. She and her husband, Guillermo, live as caretakers in a vacant hotel called Il Convento, a former convent. Hazel is trained as a preschool teacher. Her son, Juan Luis, is five. He is endearing, reserved, studious, and proud to be a kindergartener. Two-year-old Paola is a pistol. She is bursting with energy and sunshine. With her great, round, dark eyes, dark hair, and precisely cut bangs, she looks astonishingly like the TV cartoon character, Dora la Exploradora. Paola can create a game out of anything. Just hearing her laugh starts me laughing. Hazel is a lovely mother, and I adore her. She speaks Spanish slowly and clearly, as I imagine she speaks with her preschoolers, so I can understand everything she says. She knows much more English than I do Spanish, but because she learned English through reading, she is hesitant to speak. She needs help with pronunciation, and she stumbles over verb complexities, just as I do. We have abundant empathy and patience for one another.

In the little *tienda* next to my family's restaurant, I find a much-abbreviated version of *Pinocchio*, written in Spanish on one side of the page and English on the other. Hazel and I read aloud together, she in English and I in Spanish, as we help each other with pronunciation. Hazel is an incredibly fast learner. I show her how *v* is formed in the mouth differently than *b*, and how *th* is formed differently than *d*. Immediately she's got it. After a few weekly visits, Hazel asks if I would like to come by every day. I would. Whenever I arrive at Il Convento, stepping over the low cement wall that borders the hotel and walking through the underbrush to their apartment, Paola shouts, "*La señora, la señora!*" Once I meet Hazel and her family, my loneliness disappears.

A high point in my Samara sojourn is the chance to lead a discussion on *matrimonio* and *machismo* with a group of local women. I jump at the opportunity when a fellow traveler mentions that in a nearby pueblo, a *tica* named Ramona helps local women build solar ovens and leads discussions on women's issues. The traveler can't remember the name of the pueblo, just that it has a blue church. A school staff member offers to drive me there. We easily find the blue church and the house with the solar ovens. Filling the front yard is an assortment of metal-lined boxes with glass tops. They work like slow cookers, using the sun's energy. In the developing world, solar ovens offer an alternative to the open fires that damage women's eyes and lungs and frequently shorten their lives.

I introduce myself to Ramona, admire her oven project, and explain my interest in learning about marriage and couple relationships in Costa Rica. I mention that I'm a psychotherapist and happy to share what I've learned about successful marriages. Ramona responds without hesitation; she will organize a group of women to meet with me next week.

I am thrilled. After dinner at the restaurant, I begin looking up the Spanish words I may need: *couples, marriage, relationships, children, alcohol,* and *violence*. I prepare a set of introductory discussion questions and list relevant findings of current marital research. Next, I ask the school's academic director, Victor, if he will accompany me and assist with translation. Victor is the ideal choice, culturally, linguistically, and personally. He has lived in the United States and Costa Rica; he speaks Spanish and English; and he has been single, married, and divorced. He agrees to come with me.

The following week, Victor and I travel by local bus to the village with the blue church. At Ramona's house, ten women show up, a few at a time, and settle into the circle of chairs on her covered veranda. They are dressed simply and appear strong and straightforward.

Our *charla* (talk) is a lively one. When the conversation grows intense and all the women start talking at once, Victor explains what they are saying. He supplies the missing words when I respond to questions. He is particularly helpful when the husbands drive by, standing up in their jeeps and calling out to him, "What are they talking about?" Victor replies playfully, "It's a secret."

My friend Hazel has advised me to abandon my discussion questions in favor of a much simpler format. I'm grateful for her advice as I nervously begin in my rudimentary Spanish. "Let's go around the circle and each say one positive word about marriage."

Love, companionship, respect, and *dialogue* are words that come up. When I ask them to say one negative word about marriage, the first woman responds, "Machismo."

"What about other words?"

"That says it all!" the women retort almost in unison. After much laughter, they agree to go around the circle again. This time, they add *betrayal, infidelity, violence, laziness,* and *lying.*

"Can you please help me understand exactly what *machismo* means?"

The women glance at each other. I imagine they are assessing how much they are going to reveal. A plump woman sitting next to me starts. "Men believe it is the women's job to cook, clean, raise the children, work, and not expect any help from their husbands."

The woman across the circle adds, "The men make all the decisions. About money, work, the home, and children. We are supposed to obey them."

"And not have any opinions," a younger woman chimes in. "If we have an opinion, they say we are arguing."

After this, a middle-aged woman comments, "*And* we're supposed to have sex whenever they want."

What I am hearing leads me to another question. "In *tico* marriages, are men and their wives friends?"

Clearly, I've brought up a hot topic. The volume increases; the conversation accelerates. I can't follow it, so Victor explains. "They are saying their husbands' friendships with other men are way more important to them than their relationships with their wives."

Only one wife in the group describes a truly happy marriage. "My husband is my friend. He is glad to help with the children and house chores." She pauses. "The other men tease him and say he must have a very bossy wife." Later, I'll learn that this progressive husband is Ramona's son.

Listening to this lively conversation, I think about Charley and feel a surge of appreciation. Over the course of our marriage, he has come a long way as a marriage partner.

Now I ask a final question. "Do you see this machismo changing over time?"

"*Sí, pero como una tortuga.*" (Yes, but at the pace of a turtle.) At the end of the gathering, Ramona takes a group photo. But instead of saying "queso" (cheese), we all cheer, "*¡Viva la tortuga!*"

On the way home, Victor confirms what I've heard from these women. He was intrigued by the group discussion, and he seems proud of me for managing it.

In the evening, I sit at a computer at the internet café. No thunder tonight—good. I write.

"Charley, thank you for being my friend. Thank you for honoring my adventure and my separate self. Thank you for keeping on growing as a man and as a husband."

The next day, when I report back to the class—in Spanish, of course—Melvin points out that I have been speaking with rural women on the Pacific Coast where machismo is still strong. In Costa Rica's cities, things are changing. One of my classmates says, "But around here, the women work their butts off while the men sit outside together, laughing, talking, and drinking *cerveza*. How do the men justify it?" Melvin tells us with a hint of irony, "These men believe they *are* working. Their work is supervising things and protecting their women."

Each week, Victor hands out certificates of graduation to the students who are leaving. Usually, there are one or two special commendation awards given in addition to the certificates. When the school term ends for the Christmas holiday, I am amused when I receive one of them. For a moment, I wonder, *What is this? A "most improved camper" award?* Clearly, I'm not receiving it for my fluency in Spanish, so it must be for my *charla* on *matrimonia* and *machismo*.

Before I know it, it's time to leave Costa Rica for Guatemala. I donate my hammock to the school, close the gate behind me, and walk along the beach to the *calle principal* for the last time. I *so* don't want to leave this sweet community and my new friends.

On Friday night, Hazel tells me that she and her husband and children will be away from Saturday through Tuesday. I do the math and realize with a shock that this is going to be my last evening of chasing Paola around the empty swimming pool, reading books with Hazel, and playing the melon game with Juan Luis and Paola. In this game, the children crawl under the cover on the sofa; I feel their heads and bodies through the cover and wonder, "*¿Qué es esto?*" (What is this?) I feel their heads: "*¿Un melón?*" I feel their wiggly bodies: "*¿Un pavo?*" (A turkey?) Then they jump out and Paola squeals with glee at my surprise. "*¡Son niños!*" (It's children!) This will be my last night of "flying" Paola and delivering her to *aeropuertos* on the sofa, her mom's lap, or the floor. The next shock comes as I wonder how I can explain to Paola that instead of coming over every day, I am going away forever, or at least long enough to be forever to a two-year-old.

"*¿Cómo debo explicar a Paola?*" I ask Hazel. (How do I explain to Paola?)

That is when Hazel informs me that two-year-old Paola marches up to perfect strangers on the street and announces, "*La señora viene a mi casa cada dia.*" (The lady comes to my house every day.) Everywhere she goes, "*La señora viene a mi casa.*" She wakes up each morning and asks her mother, "*¿Cuándo viene la señora?*" (When is the lady coming?") While I adore the whole family, it is Paola—Paola with her enormous brown eyes, her uproarious chortles of glee, and her passion for play—who fills my heart with joy. Paola and I have fallen in love. I wish I didn't have to confuse her with my abrupt departure. I try to talk with her about needing to go away soon, but my little guru of playfulness isn't having any of it.

"Fly me like a plane again!"

CHAPTER 7

Together and Apart

GUATEMALA

*E*merging from the Guatemala City international airport, I look up and down the line of shuttle drivers holding up their signs. I spot one that says RIA SISHER. Close enough. The driver greets me and loads my luggage into his van. We drive the half hour to Antigua, and the driver delivers me to a drop-dead-gorgeous colonial estate on the outskirts of Antigua. Another adventure is about to begin.

I have arrived in Guatemala four days ahead of Charley. How charming and generous of my *esposo* to arrange such a luxurious accommodation for us. It is barely noon, and here I am in a different country and a different climate. I've exchanged the heat and humidity of Costa Rica for the Land of Eternal Spring, as Guatemala is called. Like the lucky winner on the old TV show *Queen for a Day*, I'm suddenly transported from student housing to an estate with lush gardens, a multitude of fountains, and a sparkling swimming pool. In Guatemala, fifty dollars a night can buy a lot of luxury. The room Charley and I will share has a fireplace and beamed ceiling. A vividly striped handwoven bedspread covers the supremely comfortable king-size bed. Two chairs upholstered with the same fabric face each other at the foot of the bed. What a contrast to my caved-in, worn-out mattress and sparse furnishings in Samara. Everything about Quinta de las Flores is romantic and beautiful. My eagerness for Charley to arrive grows day by day.

My favorite part of this accommodation is the pool. When I float on my back, I have a spectacular view of a towering volcano. After a bracing swim, the sun warms me as I gently swing in a brightly colored hammock. I take short walks in the vicinity of our hotel, doing my best not to get lost.

At first, the volcanoes around Antigua all look the same to me, but gradually, I can orient myself by distinguishing the smoking Volcán de Fuego to the west, Volcán de Agua to the south, and the steep volcano-shaped hills to the north. Antigua is a small and touristic colonial city with an ideal climate. It has upscale restaurants, expensive jewelry stores, interesting architecture, and irresistible *dulcerías* (sweet shops). Charley and I plan to make Antigua home base for our two weeks together, and we will make side trips from there.

As I relax at Quinta de las Flores, I anticipate my reunion with Charley. We've been apart for six weeks. This is the longest separation in our marriage. Not surprisingly, I think about making love again.

———

And that, dear readers, poses a dilemma. There is no way I can tell a story about being apart from my husband for more than a year without addressing the topic of sex. Yet I find myself facing a delicate situation. How do I balance my inclination toward candor on all subjects with my husband's predilection for privacy? *I* am the storyteller, but I'm telling a story about *our* marriage. Eventually, I recognize this as a juicy example of an issue that challenges every couple. If couples open themselves to new experiences during their marriage, they will inevitably confront their differences and need to figure out how to deal with them. For Charley and me, deciding how I will discuss sex in this book requires respectful conversations about our differing needs and wishes. And indeed, that's what we have done.

———

Cuddling has always been a big part of our love life. At home, we have a king-size bed. When our children were little, we all used to pile on the bed together, and it was the perfect size. Now we've become accustomed to a large bed, even though we only use two-thirds of it. In the years just before menopause, I had a hard time sleeping. Night sweats, middle-of-the-night trips to the bathroom, 4:00 a.m. awakenings: for the first time in my life, I understood why people who love each other might sleep in separate beds. But that isn't how it works at our house. Charley sleeps smack in the middle of our king-size bed, close enough for us to cuddle. Sometimes, when I'm feeling crowded, I tease him that he's left enough room on the other side of the bed for another woman. Occasionally, on my way back from the bathroom, I slip into the far side of the bed and whisper, "Shhh, don't tell your wife . . ."

Lying in bed at night, Charley will reach over and squeeze my sacrum. I have developed arthritis there. Charley skillfully grabs a bit of flesh and pinches it, applying the perfect amount of pressure in precisely the right spot. Alternately, he will press his fingers into the place in my hip where an inflamed sciatic nerve and a tight piriformis muscle aggravate each other like closely spaced siblings. "Ahh, perfect! You really *do* love me." Gratefully, I reach around him, find the familiar muscle knot in his shoulder, and work it. From there, I massage up and down the muscles on either side of his spine. I know from his sighs of pleasure that he, too, is feeling known and loved. It seems to me that sex in later life remains pretty much unchanged. What changes is foreplay. And the biggest change of all is what now qualifies as foreplay.

———

After four days on my own, I return to the Guatemala airport with the same shuttle driver to meet Charley. For fun, I've made a sign that reads Mi Cariño Carlito, and I've drawn big hearts all over it. I stand in line with the waiting shuttle drivers, holding my sign high above my head. I am rewarded with a fantastic grin when Charley sees me.

Once we arrive at the hotel and Charley's luggage has been delivered to our room, we both lie on the bed. "I'm scared," I confess. Charley assures me that he anticipated this. When I suggest that he let *me* make the advances, he willingly agrees. He seems to understand that I have created a shell of separateness while traveling alone. He tells me he is prepared to be patient and gentle.

With that, he drops his trousers on the floor, just as he does at home. I groan with disapproval. We both laugh.

The warmth of body against body feels lovely. But then I tense up. What's this? I feel the pulling back I learned as a teen-ager—sexually aroused yet resisting the excitement. I watch my reaction with amused curiosity. To our credit, Charley and I slip past my initial reserve and find our way back to each other.

In the morning, I compliment Charley on his staying power the night before. He confides that he has been masturbating like crazy until about a week ago, when he decided he should stop to be ready for me. He asks whether I have done the same. That's when I confess, "I've had almost no sexual urges whatsoever until about a week ago, when I began masturbating like crazy to be ready for you." We look at each other and burst out laughing.

Lying on our beautiful bed one afternoon, I ask Charley what he's been doing about his sex life in my absence. He answers, "Nothing much. Nothing exciting enough to report on."

"So, tell me about the nothing much," I press him.

Charley takes his time. "Well . . . I find myself noticing other women a lot more. It's been great for my fantasy life. So far, I don't even have to do anything—just the possibility of sexual freedom is a turn-on." I wait to see if he'll say more. Sure enough, Charley hastens to add: "But right now, my fantasies are about *you*."

———

After a few days luxuriating and exploring Antigua, Charley and I make the three-and-a-half-hour shuttle journey to Panajachel. The traffic crawls, and we breathe exhaust fumes all the way to our destination. The once-tiny and hidden-away pueblo of Panajachel, where I spent a month in 1970, no longer exists. In its place is an enormous, crowded tourist mecca. Although my friend Brad had warned me about the changes, I am shocked. We promptly head for the bustling dock in Panajachel and take a *lancha pequeña* (a sturdy but decrepit wooden boat) a third of the way around the lake to our hotel. These small outboard motorboats can transport up to twenty people, along with their produce, livestock, and textiles, to the dozen Maya pueblos around the lake.

Charley and I sit near the front of the lancha. The wave action in the afternoon causes the small vessel to smack violently against the water. Soon we are thoroughly soaked. With each bump, my body smacks resoundingly against the wooden plank on which we sit. But it doesn't diminish my joyous return to the magnificent Lake Atitlán. Later, when I'm on my own, I will learn to take the larger two-level commercial boats when the lake is rough and use the lancha only when the waves are moderate. I will know to sit toward the back of the boat near the outboard motor to avoid the hammering effect, and to position myself in the center of the hard wooden benches to avoid the spray. However, this is our first excursion, and we have yet to learn these strategies.

As our lancha pequeña carries us counterclockwise around the lake, I tap Charley's shoulder and point out the light-colored vertical stripes on the otherwise green hillsides. Those stripes are ripped-away soil from mudslides. They are why I've chosen to come back to Guatemala.

Not long after Hurricane Katrina demolished New Orleans in August 2005, Hurricane Stan took its toll on Guatemala. It was the end of the rainy season, so the ground was already saturated, and the deforested slopes of the volcanoes surrounding Lake Atitlán were especially vulnerable to mudslides. Four days of intense rain washed out the bridge that connected the twelve villages to the rest of the country. For twenty days, the Maya communities that ring the lake were cut off from clean water, food, and aid. Mudslides severely damaged houses, schools, and a hospital. It culminated in the torrential rains rupturing the steep slope of one of the volcanoes during the middle of the night. A massive mudslide entirely buried Panabaj, a tiny *pueblito* adjoining the town of Santiago Atitlán. At home in California, I read the news about these mudslides with great sadness. I wanted to help the people who lived around the lake I had once visited and come to love. From my experience as a disaster mental health volunteer with the Red Cross, I knew how traumatized the survivors must be.

Shortly before I left home, Charley told me about a child analyst whose therapeutic workbooks help children manage trauma after a major disaster. I contacted Dr. Gil Kliman and described my upcoming trip and my interest in his project. He was already customizing a version specific to Hurricane Katrina and sent me a draft of *My Story of Hurricane Katrina*. I was impressed. Coloring book pages portrayed the sequence of events in New

Orleans, and open-ended questions invited children to describe their experience. "The key to the workbook's effectiveness," Dr. Kliman explained, "is the process of doing it together with a caring adult." I proposed that while I was in Guatemala, I could adapt and translate his workbook into Spanish and make it available to the Maya children at Lake Atitlán. Dr. Kliman agreed to my proposal. I didn't mention that I would need to learn Spanish to follow through on my offer.

———

The lancha pequeña takes Charley and me to a tiny dock between two Maya villages. Staff members from the hotel welcome us at the dock and carry our suitcases up a steep flight of stone steps set into the hillside. Even relieved of our luggage, I feel the altitude of the highlands and arrive breathless at our casita, one of several perched on the steep slope.

Although I'm happy to be with Charley and admire the beautiful casita, I wish we weren't so separated from the little villages. For me, the fun of travel comes from meeting and interacting with people, not secluding ourselves in an accommodation where our privilege sets us apart. Charley's preference is for privacy, comfort, and beauty. I know he'll be happier here. I remind myself that Charley is on vacation for just two weeks. I have the rest of the year to do things my way.

Earthquake concerns keep me awake the first night. The adobe walls and heavy clay tiles of our casita arouse old fears. My vigilance about earthquakes started when I boldly moved from the Midwest to attend college in California. An earthquake would be perfect retribution for leaving my parents. Forty-three years later, I still sleep uneasily in seismically active parts of the world. Guatemala is one of those places.

In the morning, while Charley and I are enjoying Guatemalan coffee and a robust breakfast, I ask the lodge owner about the construction of the casitas. He explains that the roof tiles are made from rebar-enforced Styrofoam, currently the lightest and best material for seismic safety. Reassured, I will sleep soundly throughout the rest of our stay.

After breakfast, we put on sturdy walking shoes and set out for a hike. Charley has thoughtfully brought our hiking poles from home, and I appreciate them as we follow a high, narrow trail that looks like a horizontal ribbon circling the hillside. I am concentrating on my footing when Charley comments that I seem cool and reserved. "Are you missing Brad?" he wonders. He knows my friend Brad and knows the importance of that "Paradise is alive and well" postcard, the one that brought me to Guatemala thirty-five years ago.

"Yes, I suppose I *do* miss Brad," I respond. "I've certainly been thinking about him. He introduced me to Central America. He also showed me what it's like to hang out for a while in another culture."

Even though my friendship with Brad was not romantic, a different husband might feel jealous. I am fortunate that Charley is not a jealous guy. He listens and responds with understanding, "Of course you would miss him at Lake Atitlán."

"I also miss being twenty-six," I add.

I am thinking about my first trip as I periodically look down at the spectacular views of the lake. Brad and I didn't hike from village to village, so I never saw the lake from above. The conflict that would become a thirty-six-year civil war was heating up, and walking between villages was not safe. Returning to Lake Atitlán with Charley is a poignant blending of past and present, of old memories and new, of being single and long married, of being young and far from young—all of it connected by the exquisite beauty of the lofty volcanoes, the deep blue water, and the diamonds of sunshine glittering on the waves. Stopping on the trail, I look at my sturdy, fit husband. I am glad Charley and I are creating a whole new set of memories: our shared experience of Lake Atitlán.

In addition to introducing Charley to one of the most beautiful places on Earth, I have another purpose. I hope that visiting the various villages and seeing the storm damage will help me decide where to do my workbook project. We agree to investigate Santiago Atitlán, San Pedro, and San Marco. I already know touristy Panajachel is out of the question.

Later in the day, we take the lancha from our cliffside hotel to Santiago Atitlán. This is one of the largest villages on the lake. It is less a tourist destination than a hardworking Maya community. When we arrive at the landing pier, we notice an older man in traditional Maya garb. He is wearing embroidered knee-length pants and a red-and-black woven shirt. Around the lake, the clothing worn in each community has its own identifying colors and design. The dignified man approaches and offers his services as an official guide. We accept. The gentleman escorts us up a steep street and through the business district of a lively, colorful, and crowded community. At our request, he agrees to show us the destruction from *la tormenta* Stan. Our first shock is the sight of Hospitalito Atitlán. Buried under nearly forty feet of rock-hard mud, all that's visible is part of the third floor and the top half of a large painted red cross.

Further on, we walk past half-buried one-room houses. Clusters of makeshift crosses mark the places where entire families were buried under an avalanche of mud. This is Panabaj, one of Santiago Atitlán's poorest neighborhoods, located precariously on that unstable slope. Our guide tells us that the survivors are living in temporary shelter. Perhaps I've found the right place for my volunteer work. Then our guide mentions that there are no language schools in Santiago Atitlán. This is a serious setback. But it's also evidence that Santiago Atitlán is no tourist town.

The following day, we visit San Pedro. Our guidebook informs us that San Pedro has several language schools. (Brad has suggested that San Pedro might feel like Panajachel in the 1970s—not so.) Within minutes of our lancha's arrival, I experience strong visceral aversion. The hippie vibe is a harsh one; it overwhelms the Maya presence with the aroma of marijuana, body odor, and loud reggae music. This expat community must shock the Maya, and I imagine the two cultures do their best to ignore one other. After an hour of walking through San Pedro, I am ready to leave.

On our last full day at the lake, we head for San Marco. Large white stripes on the hills above this community suggest it also suffered severe mudslides. From our hotel, we catch a lancha pequeña crowded with *naturalezas* (indigenous people) returning from work in Panajachel late in the afternoon. Some of the passengers nod off to sleep on the water taxi after their long day of physical labor. The passengers who are awake watch us with mild curiosity. Charley and I notice we are the only foreigners onboard. I try out my Spanish with the woman seated next to me, using a mixture of very basic Spanish and pantomime to communicate. The women next to her join in. Soon we become a foursome: three Maya women and me chattering and laughing as we do our best to converse. Charley doesn't engage people as readily as I do, but he is full of smiles as he watches.

When we get to San Marco, the area near the dock exudes a New Age feel. There are bulletin boards with notices about yoga classes and spiritual healers. It is quiet here, and the vibe is mellower than Panajachel or San Pedro. As we walk through the pueblo, we can see evidence of the mudslide: rips in the hillside, a damaged school. "Maybe this is where I'd like to be when you go home," I tell Charley. "I feel comfortable here."

Our next destination was supposed to be the colorful market village of Chichicastenango. Food poisoning disrupts that plan. This is the third time I've been sick in a month. Despite being careful about my food choices and drinking only bottled water, I keep getting parasites. (By the time I leave Guatemala, I am on familiar terms with the pharmacist in Antigua. Whenever I enter the pharmacy, he greets me with, "Señora Fisher, what did you eat this time?")

As soon as the stomach cramps begin, I know I'm in for several days of intense pain, so we return to Antigua. During that time, Charley joins a guided day hike up one of the volcanoes. Among the hikers is an American family with two teenage children. Charley learns that the father is the Centers for Disease Control's chief of Foodborne and Diarrheal Diseases. Charley invites the doctor and his family to join us for dinner. I am grateful that my hero husband has returned from his hike with a world expert on the foodborne illnesses that are causing me such misery.

As I sip broth that evening, I am full of questions. The physician, who is in Guatemala to do research, explains that from the moment Guatemalan babies are weaned, they're subjected to one parasitic or bacterial infection after another. "During their critical, formative years," he explains, "the children who are lucky enough to survive suffer frequent diarrhea. That means they don't get the nutritional benefit of their food." He suggests that this may contribute to the small stature of the Maya people. I can hardly bear to imagine a tiny child repeatedly experiencing the excruciating cramps I have just been through.

After dinner, we thank the doctor and his family for joining us. What an interesting and happy family they are. Walking back on cobblestone streets toward our hotel in the dark, I think about our own family. Our son is doing research on safe water; our daughter is pursuing a career in public health; Charley is reaching out to connect with new people; I am finally exploring the world with an eye toward service. Perhaps we, too, are an interesting and happy family. I tug on Charley's arm, and when he turns toward me, I give him a long hug.

Charley suggests that during the second week of his visit, we go to Tikal to see the pre-Colombian ruins. I am fine with that plan; I'd like to learn something about the powerful Inca culture that so mysteriously disappeared. Little do I know that our tourist excursion will bring me one step closer to launching my project.

At 5:00 a.m. the morning after our arrival in Tikal, we wake for a guided predawn hike to one of the ancient pyramids. We hike by flashlight to the foot of an enormous stone pyramid. In total darkness we climb, one by one, up a narrow, steeply pitched ladder. I am shaking from the effort when Charley and I step off the ladder at the top. Our group sits in silence. Eventually, we are rewarded with the sounds of howler monkeys and birds as they begin to wake. Through swirling clouds of mist, a previously invisible second pyramid mysteriously emerges directly across from us. Next comes an unforgettable jungle sunrise. I look over at Charley and see the amazement in his eyes. This is what I've longed for: a companion who will sit with me in moments like these, feeling awe at the beauty of the natural world.

Back at the lodge, Charley and I share a breakfast table with two people from our hike, an American woman and her young adult daughter. We learn that the younger woman has just completed her Peace Corps assignment in Guatemala and is now traveling with her mother. I mention my workbook project and my uncertainty about where to stay on Lake Atitlán. The young woman replies, "If you decide to stay in Santiago Atitlán, I have a lovely friend who lives there. She's also a Peace Corps volunteer and very involved with the schools there." What serendipity! Our breakfast companion offers to email her friend and make an introduction. A few days later, I hear from Amanda. She will gladly find me a host family if I wish. She instructs me to phone her when I arrive in Santiago Atitlán. Now if I can just locate a language school . . .

From Tikal, Charley and I return to our base at Quinta de las Flores for our final few days together. In spite of a lovely vacation with Charley, I'm having trouble shaking a vague feeling of heaviness that I've noticed since arriving in Guatemala. It stands in sharp contrast to the joyfulness I felt in Costa Rica, and I wonder what it's about. Certainly, I miss swimming in the warm ocean, and I also miss being actively engaged in a community. But that's not the whole story. (Even Charley's imminent departure doesn't explain it.) This is something subtle, something I can't quite identify.

I feel it especially walking through Antigua as I watch the tiny Maya women carrying piles of woven fabrics on their heads. *Oh! I think I'm reacting to something about Guatemala itself.* This is a gorgeous country with its breathtaking volcanoes and lakes, its gentle Maya people with their vibrant textiles and colorful clothing. Yet there is a pervading sadness in this culture that I've been absorbing without realizing it: a feeling coming from outside, not inside. *Of course! This country has just come through a violent thirty-six-year civil war, and those colorfully dressed indigenous people have endured devastating atrocities. Furthermore, Guatemala has a long history of exploiting indigenous workers, with backing by US business interests and government involvement in destabilizing democratic leadership. Their suffering is palpable. No wonder I feel sad. I miss the happiness of* ticos *and the playfulness of my Costa Rican language school.* Once I recognize that in this situation, the heaviness I feel inside is my way of understanding the pain of others, I feel sturdier.

Charley and I have only one more day together. It's time for me to go on with my solo sabbatical. As I pack and brace myself for losing Charley's company, quiet, self-critical thoughts come to visit. *You'll never learn to speak Spanish. You lack self-discipline.*

At first, I am puzzled. I'm the same person I was last week when I could say *poco a poco.* Then I remind myself of what

I know as a therapist. A child's mind is alive and well inside a sixty-one-year-old who knows better. The child assumes that if she *feels* bad, it's because she *is* bad. And the child inside me believes that Charley's leaving is a punishment. The grown-up in me knows better.

Charley wakes me before dawn to kiss me goodbye. As he leaves, I see him silhouetted in the doorway pulling a large suitcase. My parting image of Charley is a profile of dark against pale light.

After his quiet departure, I fall back to sleep. When I wake again, I am alone in a king-size bed. As my eyes adjust to the morning light, I take in the colorful lamps, the small pottery sculptures, the vibrant drapes and upholstered chairs. This beautiful room has been our home base during our two weeks together. But now I am by myself again.

The good news is that I am not in a panic. The bad news is that I'm awfully close to the precipice. All day yesterday, I felt it lurking as Charley and I sorted and packed our respective belongings, making sure that my new supply of medications and heavier clothes for the cooler Guatemalan climate will not exceed what I can carry. I experienced flickers of panic, even as Charley and I savored the sexiest, most passionate lovemaking we've known. It was a parfait of goodbye sex, this-is-going-to-have-to-last-us-two-months sex, please-remember-I'm-worth-waiting-for sex, and I-wish-you-wouldn't-go sex.

———

So here I am, about to leave this elegant hacienda without a firm plan and without a partner. I feel incredibly fragile as I work to regain my solo balance. Traveling with Charley has given me an overview of Antigua and some of the villages of the Guatemalan highlands. But now he is gone, and I'm faced with three challenges. I need to shift from couple status back to being a solo traveler; I need to move from vacation accommodations back to a budget homestay; and I need to decide where I'm going next.

A few blocks from our hotel is a hostel I've noticed each time Charley and I walked past. By peeking through a little window in the thick wooden door, I know there's a lush garden behind the wall. Now I ask the gracious and unusually tall Guatemalan hotel receptionist, who I've fondly nicknamed Señor Gigante, if he will assist me in phoning the hostel. To my relief, there is space in the hostel's dormitory, and I can reserve a bed for tonight. Señor Gigante also gives me the name of a respected Spanish school in Antigua. I thank him for his kindness, and still feeling a bit forlorn, I strap on my pack and carefully roll my suitcase over the cobblestones toward Hostal el Montanes.

Ten minutes later, I am guiding my suitcase through the hostel's open door into a courtyard filled with flowering plants: birds of paradise, bougainvillea, and hibiscus. A well-dressed English-speaking woman named Carmen greets me. She is the hostel's owner. The hostel is a sturdy two-story house with fragrant vines draping its patio entry. It is airy and beautiful. The dining room is furnished with rustic dark wooden tables and colorful weavings. The hostel is literally squeaky clean; my athletic shoes make a squeaking sound with every step I take across the polished dark wood floors. Upstairs are several private bedrooms and a dorm room. There are fresh flowers and striking decorative touches throughout. It feels homey.

Carmen wants to know what brings me to Guatemala. I tell her that in addition to studying Spanish, I hope to develop a workbook to support the children who survived the mudslides at Lake Atitlán. Carmen informs me that she is the human resources director for Save the Children. She thinks my idea is excellent, and she offers to connect me with some of their staff in Santiago Atitlán.

I cannot believe my good fortune. Here is another example of the serendipity that seems to be moving me forward. Time and again in the next few months, helpful contacts will appear, almost magically, just when I need them. "Yes, that sort of thing happens all the time here," other volunteers will tell me.

———

I leave my luggage at the hostel and walk past the big Catholic church toward First Avenue. A few blocks from the hostel, I discover travelers' gold: a used bookstore filled with books in English! In my rural corner of Costa Rica, there were no English books to be found. I can hardly wait to burrow down in bed at night with an engrossing novel. An American expat runs this bookstore with its adjoining café and bar. In the back is a plant-filled eating area that serves safe, tasty, and inexpensive food. I sit in the café drinking a Coca Lite and listening to reggae music. "Don't worry about a thing / Cause every little thing's gonna be all right." And so it seems.

When I return to the hostel, I am greeted by the live-in manager, Letty, and her nine-year-old son, Luis. They speak no English, so I am obliged to start using my faltering Spanish. I ask Luis if he knows which room is mine. The boy accompanies his mother upstairs and takes me to a bedroom at the back of the house next to an immaculate bathroom. He proudly shows me the three beds and three adjoining wooden lockers that are tall and narrow and remind me of high school.

Down the hall from my room is a large lounge with several sofas and a TV. As I look around this upstairs living room, Luis comes in and settles on the floor with some modeling clay figurines. After watching the boy for a few minutes, I ask if I can join him. He hands me a lump of clay, and I sit on the floor. First, I try to make a Christmas tree, having just noticed one on the TV screen. We both agree that it looks more like *un dinosaurio*. My second attempt is more successful. Meanwhile, Luis has made a clever little sword and hilt for his clay person. I gesture and ask him if he'd like to have a duel, and he replies, "*¿Grande o pequeño?*" (Large or small?) I indicate that it's his choice. "*Grande*," he decides. We take large lumps of clay and shape two daggers. Soon we are dancing around the large room, thrusting, parrying, and circling the overstuffed chairs situated in the center of the room in front of the TV. After a while, both swords look a lot like bananas, and we end up breathless and laughing.

Next, we move on to *pistolas*, and we have a lively shoot-out that grows more technical when Luis makes us each four clay bullets. The thuds of wounded bodies crashing to the floor whenever a clay ball hits its human target brings Letty upstairs. She sits in one of the stuffed chairs, placing herself near the center of the shoot-out. She smiles warmly even while clay balls hit the walls and windows and leave oily imprints on the clean glass. Luis generously shares the balls, so I always have as many as he does.

When I am worn out from diving behind sofas or dying a miserable death on the hardwood floor, I propose that we read a book that I brought from home. *Herman the Helper* was one of our son's preschool favorites. Herman is a little octopus who loves to swim around helping out his family and friends with his many arms. I selected it when I was looking for easy reading books in English. In addition to its beautiful illustrations, it reminds me that, like Herman, I really like to help.

Luis is learning English in third grade, and he is eager to read with me. First, I explain Herman's story as best I can in my simple Spanish while we look together at each colorfully illustrated page. Then I read him the story in English: "Herman liked to help. He helped his mother. He helped his father." And finally, Luis echoes me as we read the book together.

On another evening, I bring out a plastic inflatable globe from my kid kit, and we kick it around the upstairs hall for a while. Like most Guatemaltecos, Luis is crazy about *fútbol*, a.k.a. soccer. He quickly names our noisy evening activity "globo-fútbol." After a while, I help him locate California and Guatemala. Amazed, he informs his mother, "*¡Mama, Guatemala es pequeño!*" (Mama, Guatemala is small!)

The Monday after I move from Quinta de las Flores to the hostel, I enroll in the Spanish language school that Señor Gigante recommended. I may want to travel back and forth between Antigua and Santiago Atitlán. Antigua has well-trained teachers who can help me correct and edit my workbook translation, and Santiago Atitlán is where the largest shelter for displaced mudslide victims is situated. It's also where I now have the promise of a homestay and professional contacts for my project.

It is quite a long walk from my hostel in Antigua to the language school at the opposite end of town. I had intended to spend only a few nights at this hostel before arranging a more permanent homestay, but after several days, as I settle under the warm covers of a fine, firm bed in the dorm room I have all to myself, I think about kind, maternal Letty and playful Luis, and I know that I've already found my homestay.

Breakfast is included in my room fee. I wake up each day to the sound of birds singing their hearts out through the open window of my room. En route to the bathroom, I look out at cathedral domes, tile rooftops, and a volcano through the long wall of glass in the upstairs hallway. Supper is a bonus: special time in the kitchen helping Luis with math homework while Letty cooks us refried beans and eggs and serves them with fresh bread from the *panadería* down the street.

A few weeks into my stay, Doña Letty asks me how old I am. I am curious to know why. Apparently, Carmen phoned the hostel one day and, overhearing me playing with Luis, she'd asked Letty, "What in the world is that racket?" Letty explained it was just their guest having a shoot-out with Luis. So now Letty wants to know how old I am. When I tell her I am sixty-one, Letty replies with astonishment, "Well you certainly don't *act* your age!"

During the next year, I will visit several continents, meet many people, live with quite a few families, and hear a variety of observations about myself. But of all the feedback I receive throughout my travels, this one will remain my most treasured compliment.

CHAPTER 8

Giving Back

GUATEMALA

*A*s soon as our *lancha* approaches the pier in Santiago Atitlán, a skinny youngster comes racing to meet the boat. Although others are loudly competing for my attention, this energetic boy is the first to offer his services as a porter.

Living at the hostel with Luis and Letty and attending language school occupies half my time. The other half is spent in the large Maya community of Santiago Atitlán on the shores of Lake Atitlán in the Guatemalan highlands.

Charley and I were together on my most recent visit to Lake Atitlán. This time, I am on my own. I remember how steep Santiago's main street is, and now I have luggage. We negotiate a fee, and then I ask the boy his name; he is Gregorio. Before going anywhere, I need to phone Amanda, the Peace Corps volunteer who lives in Santiago Atitlán. She has, hopefully, arranged a homestay for my remaining months in Guatemala. Gregorio guides me to a tienda near the pier where, for a few quetzals—the local currency—I phone Amanda. She instructs me to walk up the main street to a restaurant called El Pescador, saying someone from my host family will be there to greet me. I realize I am already witnessing something new and extraordinary about this culture. That I can call Amanda without having specified when I'd be coming to Santiago and she could arrange for my host to meet me in the time it takes to walk up a hill is certainly unique in my life experience.

Gregorio bravely hoists my heavy suitcase onto his shoulder, and rather than rolling it, he *carries* it up the steep hill to the central part of town. Gregorio, it turns out, is thirteen. I had guessed him to be about ten, but I'll soon learn to adjust age estimates upward, taking into account the smaller stature of the indigenous population. Out of breath from carrying just myself and a small pack, I follow my intrepid young porter up the main street past outdoor stalls whose owners urge me to *pase adelante* (come on in).

Gregorio guides me to the restaurant. A short, round Maya woman is waiting. She is dressed in a beautiful huipil top embroidered with birds and the traditional hand-woven long skirt. She introduces herself as Lolita. She leads me two or three blocks down a steep dirt road filled with potholes. Actually, "with potholes" is not quite accurate; the street itself is one giant pothole. My host family lives in a large, white, two-story stucco house in the elbow of the curving, unpaved street. As we enter the house, I find myself inside a small tienda, a snack shop with racks of Cheez-Its, Fritos, and corn nuts; a cooler with soft drinks; and cases of *pan dulce*— the sweet bread I remember so vividly from thirty-five years ago. (The Maya pronounce "*pan*" like "pahng" with a nearly silent *g*.)

Looking around, I am initially put off by the house with its concrete floors, courtyard bathroom, and barking dog. The room where I will stay has cement walls with peeling green paint and a cracked and dusty linoleum floor. It is furnished with a large, elaborately carved armoire, a desk, and a bed covered with a dusty blanket. The common bathroom is off a central courtyard; it, too, has a cement floor and walls, and it doesn't seem totally clean. I look around with some concern; I am nervous about eating food cooked in this house.

After putting my clothing away in the slightly musty armoire, I walk back up the unpaved road to the main street. Turning the corner, I locate an internet café. It has dusty but surprisingly good computers. A tall, blond German woman seated at the next computer is also living with a family in Santiago Atitlán.

"How is it?" I want to know.

"Great! My host family is terrific," she tells me.

I feel a small pang of envy. I finish my emailing and walk home for supper. When I enter my family's tiny kitchen, the same young German woman is seated happily at the kitchen table. My reaction is a mix of relief and hilarity. Life can be so funny.

My host family and their boarders quickly charm me. Lolita and Chonita are sisters. I'm guessing they are in their early forties, and they are warm and adorable. Lolita runs the tienda and does some of the cooking. Chonita sits at a table in one corner of the tienda, and her sewing machine hums all day as she works on exquisite huipil designs. It takes about three days for her to create a circle of extravagant flowers and birds all around the neck opening of a huipil. I am intrigued when I take a close look at her workspace and discover that Chonita is using Peterson's *Field Guide to Western Birds* as her reference.

The sisters speak in clear and comprehensible Spanish. Because it is their second language, they speak slowly and use simple vocabulary. With one another, they speak Tzutuhil, the local dialect of this village. The house belongs to their parents, Mercedes and Salvador, a hardworking elderly couple. The other international boarders include Christina, the German woman, and Katie, a Peace Corps volunteer from Colorado. There is also Calypse, an enormous black dog who barks ferociously at any male visitors. At night, Calypse competes to out-bark all the other dogs in the village. Nicholas is Lolita and Chonita's brother. He lives just down the road and runs a bakery that provides the fresh pan dulce that fills the tienda's glass cases. My favorite of these sweetened breads is a small, round roll with a dollop of frosting on top; it is the ultimate comfort food.

Every morning, when the roosters at the surrounding concrete block buildings wake me, I lie in my bed and listen to the rhythmic sound of Mama Mercedes slapping her palms together as she makes tortillas. Breakfast is my favorite meal. I love entering the toasty-warm kitchen, a room about the size of a suburban bathroom. Usually, Christina is already there when I show up around 7:30. I am greeted by the aroma from a pot of sugar-laden dark coffee. A small table is pushed against the wall and flanked by three red plastic stools. Located in the back corner of the room is the life of the kitchen: a wood-burning stove. It is essentially a cement enclosure with a pocket for burning kindling and, above it, a large cast-iron surface. Mama Mercedes sits on a plastic stool facing the fire with her back to us. She slaps her palms with fingers arched outward. Patting and clapping, she passes the slightly damp tortilla dough from one palm to the other. I tell her how much I love waking to the first song of the day: *la música de las tortillas.*

I regret that there's no language school in Santiago Atitlán. But I love staying with Luis and Letty at Hostal el Montanes, so I'm content to shuttle back and forth between Antigua and the lake, spending a week in each place and making the daylong pilgrimage by boat and minivan. The language schools in Antigua offer one-on-one instruction, and I've requested a teacher who can assist me in translating *My Story of Hurricane Stan.*

Thanks to Carmen, on my second day in Santiago Atitlán, I have an appointment with local representatives from Save the Children. We are to meet in front of the municipal building in Parque Central. It is a brave journey for me, with my terrible sense of direction, to make my way up the three blocks from my homestay to the market and then turn right to the municipal building. All along the way, tienda owners call out, "*Pase adalante, compra algo.*" (Come in, buy something.) I nod to the women in their traditional dress who are selling woven clothing, tote bags, and beaded jewelry. All of it is vividly colorful and enticing, but I keep walking.

When two men and a woman from Save the Children arrive, the four of us sit on a low cement wall, and I show them the original Hurricane Katrina workbook and my progress to date creating a handwritten Spanish translation. I explain the workbook's purpose: to minimize post-disaster trauma by encouraging children to tell their stories and color pictures of the event. The people from Save the Children seem enthusiastic about my project and offer to help. The woman, Celedonia, lives just four blocks from my host family, and she invites me to her home. She tells me that her roommate, Angelica, is a psychologist who works with children at three local schools.

She and Angelica live together in one large room. I can see that the tidy space functions as office, bedroom, kitchen, and dining room. They serve me more sweet coffee and pan dulce and look at the Katrina workbook. For some reason, I have great difficulty understanding their Spanish. I have to ask them to repeat just about everything two or three times. I feel discouraged that my Spanish comprehension is sometimes so inadequate. I smile a lot in compensation and hope their accents will grow more familiar as time goes on.

In a most amazing stroke of luck, I have arrived in Santiago Atitlán just as the half dozen mental health workers from different agencies decide to coordinate their efforts to serve this community in the wake of the disaster. Their first meeting will be the following morning, and Angelica invites me to attend. As I walk the few blocks back to my homestay, I marvel at the good fortune that has landed me in happy homes in two communities, provided contacts for my workbook project, and scored me an invitation to the very first meeting of a new mental health commission. My sense of being lost is certainly short-lived. I am relieved and astonished at how easily I have landed on my feet. Would it have been this easy in my twenties had I dared to embark on a global adventure of travel and service? I think it unlikely. And I would certainly have had less to offer. But it *is* happening now, and I feel grateful and receptive to whatever comes next.

The following morning, I arrive at the Centro de Salud and become a charter member of the Comisión por la Salud Mental de Santiago Atitlán. The group consists of two mental health administrators, three psychologists, another social worker, and me. I am the only non-Guatemalan present. The other participants are cordial and remarkably tolerant of my painfully slow speech. At first, I understand almost nothing, but I write down key words and look them up later. (Mobile phones are not yet in common use, but my Spanish-English pocket dictionary is always in my travel purse.)

One morning, I practice making tortillas. Mercedes offers encouragement, and soon we are bursting with laughter at my thick, misshapen tortillas with holes in them. Lolita and Chonita alternate making breakfast for Christina and me. We might have French toast made from pan dulce, or perhaps a milky gruel with warm banana slices. There is always a carafe of intensely sweet coffee. Sometimes after breakfast I massage Mama Mercedes's left shoulder, the one that is chronically sore. Supper is usually a simple meal: wonderfully fresh scrambled eggs with refried beans and tortillas. But morning is the sweetest time. The fire warms the entire room, and all of us crowd in together.

My hosts are very conscious of hygiene and gringo stomachs. I never once get sick from food prepared here. This family turns out to be one of the happiest I have ever known. Laughter is our common language, and we are all fluent in it. I am so glad I didn't let dust and crumbling plaster turn me off. Amanda knew what she was doing.

In the larger community, certain areas are poor, crowded, underserved, and lacking in hygiene or infrastructure. Santiago Atitlán is situated on the shore of one of the most beautiful lakes in the world, and yet many who live here primarily see high concrete walls, exposed rebar, road dust, and trash. From a few corners they can catch glimpses of the lake, but mostly it is obscured.

At five foot nothing, I tower over the three Maya women in my Santiago family. When Mama Mercedes inquires about my age, I tell her I'll soon be sixty-two, and from that point on she asks me about vitamins and what brand I prefer. Some days later, she mentions that she has just turned sixty-three. She easily looks ten years older than me. She wonders about the vitamins, she tells me, because I have the soft, flexible body of a thirty-year-old. I tell her gently that in fact, I have the body of a very privileged Norte Americana who has done no physical labor and had a lifetime of good nutrition and sanitary water. I am stunned to realize that the sisters I've been relating to as my peers are the *children* of the woman who is my actual peer.

Each morning after breakfast, I make my bed, open the curtains, and settle myself at the table in my room to work at translating *My Story of Hurricane Katrina* into Spanish. I love this daily activity. I look up vocabulary and make sure I'm conjugating my verbs correctly before I write on the sheets of loose-leaf paper I purchased from a little tienda. Doing Latin and French homework in high school was a lot like this, except now my efforts have an actual purpose. I work happily for several hours each day and then stop for lunch. Afterward, I walk to the internet café. This is my reward.

The experience of creating *Mi Historia de la Tormenta Stan* turns out to be an interweaving of language study, solitary translation time, and attendance at meetings devoted to coordinating relief efforts. I carry a tiny notebook and accumulate unfamiliar words that I hear at community meetings: *deslave* is "mudslide," *red de apoyo* is "support group," and *capacitación* is "training."

One afternoon in Santiago Atitlán, two local women working as home visitors invite me to accompany them while they conduct a needs assessment in the *albergue*, a refugee camp of plastic tarps set up to shelter the survivors of la tormenta Stan. Rosario and Magdalena are part of a special project for mothers and children. I readily accept the invitation, and the three of us go doorway to doorway (there *are* no doors; just flaps) as Rosario and Magdalena interview the residents of the albergue in Tzutuhil, their indigenous dialect. People are cold at night. They are crowded. Their children are getting sick from foodborne illnesses. The poverty and squalor are beyond belief, set against the backdrop of towering volcanoes and a breathtaking lake. Above all, people are frightened because the temporary shelters have been erected directly in the path of the killer mudslide.

Rosario is considerate and explains to me in slow, clear Spanish after each interview what has been discussed in Tzutuhil. When I ask if my presence is a problem, she assures me that on the contrary, it is advantageous to have me along. Rosario explains that my being a Norte Americana lends credibility to their efforts, making it easier to obtain information and take photographs for the needs assessment.

The concern on everyone's mind, disaster victims and relief workers alike, is that the shelters—flimsy wooden frames covered with plastic sheeting—will be swimming in mud when the rains come just a few months from now.

Next, we climb a steep hillside to Panabaj, where the poorest of Santiago's poor live in one-room hovels that inexplicably escaped the mudslide. In the yard of one house, Rosario points out a child of about sixteen months. The little girl has the telltale bulging belly and reddish tint to her hair that are indicative of malnutrition. Since the other children in this family look adequately fed, I suspect she isn't eating because of pain from parasites or an untreated bacterial infection. The children in Panabaj are barefoot and unbathed; their mothers look worn and old. Their homes have dirt floors and are made of sticks. These dwellings have no doors, so chickens wander freely in and out.

We visit another somewhat less impoverished neighborhood to do interviews. I notice a group of young girls playing behind a fort of blankets. On closer examination, I realize they aren't playing; they are doing beadwork to sell to tourists. Unlike the boys, who are indeed playing, these little girls, no older than seven or eight, are already part of the labor force. It's sad to see such contrasting roles so early in the lives of these children.

It is stimulating to be out among the people of Santiago Atitlán, but I love coming back to my family's house at the end of each day. At sundown, a parade of small children comes through the tienda, clutching coins for a bag of chips or a *choco-banano*, a skewered frozen banana that's been dipped in melted chocolate and then returned to the freezer.

Morning and evening, the streets fill with smoke from the wooden cooking fires as the women prepare food. I have the best view of this scene from the flat roof of my family's house, where we go to do laundry. I hand-wash my clothes in the cement outdoor sink and hang them to dry on the rooftop clothesline. When I slip on my nightshirt at bedtime, sometimes it smells like fresh air and sunshine, and sometimes it smells like a campfire.

The contrast between my lifestyles in Antigua and Santiago Atitlán is apparent in the smallest details. Letty keeps the Hostal el Montanes so clean that I walk barefoot to the bathroom next to my bedroom. In Santiago Atitlán, I wear flip-flops and step gingerly in the dark to avoid tripping on cracked cement and to evade the patrolling dog as I visit the courtyard *baño* several times a night. Eventually, I will buy a plastic bowl with a lid and use it as a chamber pot till morning.

The differences between my homestays in Antigua and Santiago Atitlán reflect an overall discrepancy between the lives of *los ladinos*, those of European ancestry, and those of *los indígenas*, the historically oppressed native population. Antigua is a city filled with tourists and expats and well-to-do Guatemalans. Santiago Atitlán is a Maya pueblo; it is reputed to be the largest community of Maya in Latin America. Although my accommodations in Santiago are humble, when I show my teacher in Antigua some photos of my Santiago host family, she points out their leather shoes, the metal griddle on their wood-burning stove, and the elaborately carved armoire in my room. Based on these observations, she informs me that I am definitely living with a well-to-do Maya family.

During my early weeks in Santiago Atitlán, I repeatedly embarrass myself by mistaking one traditionally garbed Maya person for another. One of the social workers invites me to accompany her to a training session for local midwives. Even though it is conducted in Tzutuhil and I comprehend nothing, I am fascinated to encounter the women who deliver many of the community's babies. At a mental health commission meeting the next day, I warmly thank the social worker for bringing me along. She gives me a blank look and then graciously accepts my thanks. A few minutes later, in walks the woman who actually took me to the training session the previous day. I turn beet red, and my face is still hot at the end of the meeting. On another occasion, I address one of the social workers as "Angelica" until she finally tells me, "I am Lucia; I don't know anyone named Angelica." Once again, I am mortified. Must I constantly reveal that all Maya look alike to me?

Then one day, the youngest of the four children in my host family comes to visit for the weekend. Diana is twenty-six years old and the only member of her family who speaks English. She lives and works in Guatemala City. Walking into the cozy kitchen and seeing me for the first time, she greets me warmly with "Hello, Katie." I return her greeting with a straight face, but I can hardly contain my mirth. Here I am, sixty-something, gray-haired, barely five feet tall, and petite. Katie is twenty-three years old; she is a towering five ten with curly blond hair, a loud booming voice, and the strong, athletic body of a former college swimmer.

Suddenly, I get it. It's not just me. To a Maya person, all *gringas* look alike. Diana's faux pas helps me relax and forgive myself until, little by little, I get to know people in town well enough to keep them straight.

———

Each day, as I walk past the outdoor stalls with their vivid array of beaded handicrafts and woven fabric, the women call out, "*¡Pase adelante, compre algo, buen precio!*" (Come in, buy something, good price!) I politely reply each time, "*Buenos días, Señora*" or "*Buenas tardes, Señorita*," and add that I am living with a family here in Santiago. No matter: the next time I walk by, it is the same: "*¡Pase adelante, buen precio!*" One morning, after five weeks of this ritual, I walk by the stalls on my way to a meeting, and to my amazement, a young woman greets me with "*Buenos días.*" Other women overhear and soon follow suit. Now, finally, I have the pleasure of exchanging greetings whenever I pass these tourist stalls. I am so glad I chose to stay in one place long enough to be recognized as a person and not just a potential buyer of souvenirs.

———

My commute back and forth between Antigua and Santiago Atitlán is a grueling five-hour journey each way that includes congested roadways, choking exhaust fumes, and a choppy boat ride across a huge lake. Still, it's worth it to see Letty and Luis and work on my translation with a skilled native speaker. I find a teacher who is smart and flexible and genuinely interested in my project. We spend intense and productive days going over each section of the workbook, correcting and improving my translation line by line.

I have now been in Guatemala for almost eight weeks. After returning to Santiago Atitlán, I distribute copies of the handwritten workbook to my mental health commission colleagues. They help review it for grammar, content, and cultural sensitivity. During my time in Santiago, I network with as many organizations as I can. I enjoy the double benefit of getting to know people in the community while laying the groundwork for implementing the workbook once I've left. The response has mostly been supportive and enthusiastic. Local residents step up to help. Alvaro, the manager of the internet café, lets me use one of his computers to work on the book whenever they are not too busy. This is his contribution to the *proyecto*.

———

One day, I hear on the street that a group of seven mental health students is in town. In true Santiago fashion, I run into the seven women a short while later near the *albergue*. They are graduate students from a university in Guatemala City. They appear to be in their thirties, and they are clearly upper-class Guatemalans: well-dressed and attractive. To my dismay, they inform me that they are doing a pilot project, helping the children and adults work through their trauma by telling their stories of Tormenta Stan. Inwardly, I am screaming, "Stop! That's *my* project!" But what I actually say is, "How interesting. In fact, I am translating and adapting an activity book for the same purpose. Perhaps we can work together." Karin and I exchange phone numbers. When I call, Karin suggests I join them the following afternoon. It turns out I needn't have worried. A weeklong exchange of professional skills, mutual interests, and friendship is about to begin.

In the morning, I ride from the center of town toward the Posada de Santiago in the back of a pickup truck filled with Maya workers. After climbing carefully out of the truck and paying the driver the equivalent of a quarter, I look around and locate an imposing stone house just past the Posada. It stands out in contrast to the crumbling stucco homes of the indigenous population. Feeling a little shy, I climb the uneven stone steps up to the front entrance. Before lifting the knocker on the thick wooden door, I turn to savor the spectacular view of the lake. I never cease to find this vista breathtaking: the enormous lake in its many moods, the majestic volcanoes. Several *cayucos* are out on the lake this morning. In each carved canoe, a fisherman stands and lifts his paddle from one side to the other as he skillfully propels his vessel back to shore. Below me, children shout as they exuberantly jump off the hotel's wooden dock into the cold lake. For now, this intriguing community hugging the shore of Lake Atitlán is my home.

Karin responds to my knock, welcomes me into her home, and introduces me to each of the women. They are members of a new master's program in Counseling and Mental Health at a university in Guatemala City. Several are fluent in English, and all of them are delightfully welcoming and warm. I am intrigued as they describe the experiential learning situations they have choreographed for the women and children of the *albergue*.

On the first day of their activities, the students divide into two groups. One group, led by a rosy-cheeked woman named Marta, engages the children in building a volcano. From preschool age to young teens, the children scramble to bring the requested items: rocks and branches and pebbles and sand. They build their volcano with gusto. Girls carry their dusty, sometimes crying baby siblings on their backs as they work. Little boys get excited and a bit wild, throwing rocks and dirt and water onto the construction. The social work students wisely modify their plan so that *they* orchestrate the actual mudslide. They ask the children what they heard, saw, thought, felt, and wondered during the mudslide. Two nine-year-old girls who are living in the temporary shelter take turns translating the social workers' questions from Spanish to Tzutuhil for the younger children who haven't yet learned Spanish.

The following day, the social workers will help the children use natural materials to reconstruct their destroyed village. We note with interest that the first structure the children ask to rebuild, even before their homes or their school, is a church.

While these social work students are involved with the children, the other group conducts an intense and dramatic activity for the adult women of the shelter. Karin is the spokesperson, and although the participants are all women, their translator is Diego, a man who appears to be a respected elder among the Maya. I am fascinated as Karin conducts a riveting and powerful activity to help the large group of women seated on blankets on the ground explore their feelings of grief and depression. She has brought with her an abundance of colorful chiffon scarves. "Each color," she explains, "can represent a feeling." As she holds up each colored scarf, she pairs it with a feeling. "Yellow could be for happiness; green might be for curiosity; blue could be peacefulness; red might be anger; pink could be contentment; white could be fear; and gray could be sadness." Karin pauses for effect. "When a dreadful event like a *deslave* comes along, it can leave us with such a heavy heart that it covers all these other feelings with a black cloud of depression."

Karen has found a dramatic way to convey the experience of depression. She brings out a large black chiffon scarf and lays it over the colored scarves. "If the black cloud is heavy enough, it may be hard to experience any of the other feelings we possess." Karin doubles and triples the black scarf so that each time it is folded, the scarf becomes increasingly opaque. "Sometimes we feel tied up in a tight knot of depression." Karin wraps up all the colored scarves under the black scarf and ties them into a tight bundle. "This can make us ill. When this happens, we need medicine to make us well again."

"And that medicine," Karin goes on to explain with Diego translating one phrase at a time, echoing Karin's dramatic tone and emphatic pauses, "that medicine is to tell our stories to people who will listen and care. When we tell our stories of what happened to us, when we share our experiences and our feelings with others in our community, that is the medicine that removes the dark cloud and lets us get our feelings back." Karin lifts the black scarf off the bundle. What she does next is masterful. She begins to throw down each of the brightly colored scarves, stand-ing next to it as she names the emotion it represents. Standing by the blue scarf, she says, "As we are healing, we might feel peace-ful. And if we feel it, *está bien*; it is OK." Karin throws down the yellow scarf. "We might feel happy. And if we feel it, *está bien*." One by one, she stands beside each scarf. "We might feel sad. And if we do, *está bien*. We might feel angry, perhaps very, very angry. And if we do, *está bien*."

The seated women, many of them holding babies or small children, watch Karin with eyes riveted. She pauses again and again while Diego translates, skillfully matching her delivery as well as her words. The attunement between them, two people whose lives would never ordinarily intersect, amazes me. And soon the stories flow. A mother recounts losing all fourteen of her children in one devastating night; a grandmother cannot understand why or accept that she was spared while her children and grandchildren perished.

In an indigenous culture where feelings and emotions are rarely identified or discussed, this activity offers a powerful teaching for the women. It provides an important teaching for the mental health students as well. These wealthy, privileged women have never known an individual Maya person. One social work student says as much. "I've come here for years but never once had a personal interaction. I only saw an indistinct mass of poor indigenous people." Humbled by the experiences of the week, her eyes have been opened, bringing newfound interest in and respect for the individuals she has met.

After each day's activities, we return to Karin's house, where we debrief and prepare for the next day's activities.

The week I've spent with these remarkable women has benefited all of us. I'm grateful for the vitality and warmth they have brought to the mudslide survivors and to me. Apparently, the appreciation is mutual. The social work students find a wonderful way to thank me for my involvement. They decide to share the task of doing final edits on the Spanish draft of my workbook. Each woman takes a portion of the book to check the grammar and vocabulary and correct any other errors. By the next day, I have a fully edited workbook. What a beautiful gift.

———

After the social work students leave Santiago Atitlán, I get the blues. I've loved being part of their circle. I miss them and feel quite lonely—something I haven't experienced much on my Guatemala adventure. I decide to invite Letty and Luis to join me for the weekend at the Posada de Santiago. This will be their first visit to Lake Atitlán. I meet them in Panajachel, and together, we cross the lake. I escort them to the rustic stone hotel and restaurant. Across the road is an aging swimming pool, canoes, and a makeshift hot tub right on the waterfront. Luis has his first experience of swimming, and I get to witness him falling in love with my favorite sport.

"Doña Leah, this is *buenísima!*" exclaims my young friend.

During their visit, I find out that the hotel also has a low-cost dormitory. As much as I love my Santiago host family, I know that being close to the water's edge on this magnificent lake will boost my sagging spirits. I move into the dorm at the Posada for my final week in Santiago Atitlán.

I continue to visit my host family every day, but my move turns out to be just the right medicine. The walk back and forth into town provides much-needed exercise after weeks of sitting and writing. On evenings when I am tired, I pay my quarter and jump onto one of the pickup trucks crowded with *indígenas*. I love being part of this group all smooshed together, hanging onto the overhead bars as the truck lurches over the bumpy road. Their striking clothes and glossy black hair are intensified by the setting sun.

The workbook is nearly finished. A month earlier, I hired a Maya artist living in Santiago Atitlán to create the coloring book illustrations. I want the drawings to depict the disaster and the process of recovery. Although the artist is talented, he has required a great deal of motivating. Every few days, I walk to his house to check on his progress. Most often there is none. If he's not at home, I wait on the sunny steps by the gate to his house. When he returns, I greet him and his wife warmly. I remind him that the book is nearly finished and that I will be leaving Guatemala and going home in a few weeks. I express effusive delight with every successive page as he completes it. Indeed, each one is a gorgeous line drawing, perfect for children to color. There is a detailed drawing of the volcano and Santiago Atitlán before the disaster, a drawing of the mudslide itself, a picture of parents and children separated, and another of families reunited. There is a perfect rendition of the emergency shelters and a final hopeful drawing of the corn growing back with children once again at play.

Soon I will need funds to pay the artist and a typist and to cover printing costs for copies of the book. I attempt to get funding from some of the American NGOs already serving the community. I spend long hours in the internet café writing proposals, stopping just for meals. As it becomes clear that this application process will be slow and uncertain, I turn to my own network of friends and family. Emailing the eighty-four people on my sabbatical pen pal list, I describe the workbook project and invite small contributions. Within ten days, I have a budget of $1,300 for *Mi Historia de la Tormenta Stan*.

There's no way I could have done *this* in the Peace Corps. Although I regret having passed up the chance to travel and be of service when I was younger, I am grateful for the freedom I have now to act independently. I'm glad I'm not limited by rules and regulations, that I'm able to find my own solutions. With the funds from my friends, the project can now move forward. Perhaps once the workbook is completed and distributed, one of the NGOs will recognize its usefulness and get involved. In fact, that is precisely what will happen, but I don't know this yet.

In an email to Charley, I write, "I feel so fully alive. I haven't felt this alive since our babies were born and I was the mother of young children; since the days when they would argue over who got to hold the hand with my wedding ring." He writes back that he is delighted for me and incredibly proud.

Charley and I are both surprised by how close we feel during our separation. Absent the annoyances of daily living together, our loving and romantic feelings become dominant. Disagreements and disappointments fade into the background. So far, it doesn't seem that my long journey has harmed our marriage in any way. (Of course, Charley has not taken me up on my offer regarding recreational sex. I wonder how I would feel if he ever did.)

As the culmination of my project and the end of my time in Guatemala draws near, I arrange a farewell fiesta at the Posada de Santiago to thank the people in the community who have supported and participated in the book project. I invite the artist who made drawings for the coloring book; Alvaro from the internet café; my Santiago family; Mario, who typed up the manuscript; the Peace Corps volunteers Amanda and Katie; and the members of our Santiago mental health commission. Knowing that flowery speeches are expected in this culture, I labor for days over my farewell speech, dictionary in hand. If I needed further evidence that I'm living in a very different culture, I extend nineteen invitations three days prior to the luncheon, and nineteen people are free to attend. At home, given a month's notice, two-thirds of my friends would already be busy.

I am far from a confident hostess, even with someone else doing the cooking. On the day before my departure from Santiago, I nervously greet my guests as they straggle into the picturesque restaurant around noon. Hot-off-the-press copies of *Mi Historia de la Tormenta Stan* are at each place. When most of the guests have arrived, I shyly stand and welcome them. After the meal, I stand again to offer my Spanish thank-you speech, looking up often as I read slowly and, hopefully, clearly.

"I came to Guatemala with three purposes. I wanted to learn Spanish, I wanted to know if someone my age could be useful in the world, and I wanted to find out if I could travel alone feeling safe and happy."

I look up and see the family and friends I've made and continue.

"I discovered that 'traveling alone' does not exist. It is only an idea. Alone is the moment before making contact on the phone with Amanda, the moment before meeting Lolita, Chonita, Salvador, and Mercedes, my family in Santiago Atitlán. Alone is the moment before joining the mental health commission, and the moment before working on this book together with all of you. 'Traveling alone' does not exist. It is simply a big jump of faith."

Then I tell them, "I have achieved my three goals. I can now speak very bad Spanish without fear; I know for sure that I can travel on my own and be safe and happy; and I know that when I work together with people like you, I can be useful in the world."

The following day, I kiss my Santiago family goodbye and take the lancha and shuttle back to Antigua. Luis is filled with sadness about my departure. He wants to stay home from school to see me off. I promise him that I will return, that our friendship is important to me, and that I want to watch him grow.

I have one final mission before I go home. Someone encouraged me to give a copy of *Mi Historia de la Tormenta Stan* to Ignacio Ochoa, the director of Nahual Foundation in Antigua. They described him as a remarkable man: a former Jesuit, a Guatemalan Civil War activist, and now a dedicated and effective community organizer. Our meeting is scheduled for my last evening in Antigua.

It is dark as I hurry along the cobblestone streets to my appointment at the Fundación Nahual office. When I knock, a man with a kind face and modest manner answers the door and leads me to a large room with worn sofas and a rustic, carved conference table. Once seated at the table, I use my limited vocabulary and creative verb endings to explain my reason for meeting with him. "I am from the United States, and I know a psychiatrist in America who helps children after a disaster. He made a workbook, and I came to Guatemala to translate it from English to Spanish. In Santiago Atitlán, I discovered an artist to make pages for children to color." Beside me, Ignacio sits perfectly still as he listens patiently to my halting Spanish. I reach into my travel purse again and again to look up new or forgotten words in the tiny pocket dictionary. I describe my project and show Ignacio the completed workbook. Together we lean over it, and he slowly turns the pages of the coloring book section. Ignacio points to the drawing of Lake Atitlán and comments in clear, measured Spanish. "Yes, I recognize the buildings; this is the Posada de Santiago." He thoughtfully examines each drawing: the mudslide, the half-buried houses, the child dreaming in his bed made from tree limbs. He touches the drawing of the bed and smiles. "When I was a child, I had a bed exactly like that one." We admire the optimistic picture of an anticipated recovery, with homes being rebuilt, children rolling hoops, and the *milpa* (corn) growing tall again. I ask, "Do you think this book might be useful to the children?"

Ignacio responds with calm conviction. "I am certain this book can be very useful. Several pueblos close to Antigua were severely affected by the storm. The children there are frightened and anxious. Without some intervention, the next rainy season will be terrifying for them." Listening to Ignacio, I feel hopeful. Here is someone who seems to understand and care. My hopefulness turns into excitement when he adds, "Because I work with the communities, I know some teachers who will be very interested in these workbooks."

I give Ignacio a copy of *Mi Historia de la Tormenta Stan* and prepare to leave. When I mention I'll be flying back to the United States in the morning, Ignacio stands and addresses me with the dignity of an ambassador: "I wish to thank you for your efforts on Guatemala's behalf."

I can't imagine a more perfect farewell.

CHAPTER 9

Intermezzo

ARIZONA

I'm home! I am here for two months: ample time to get together with our children and special friends, time for several trips to see my mother, and time to remind Charley he's a happily married man.

I am excited to be back. The spring garden is waking up. The blue and lavender irises have just opened. Yellow fruit weighs down our lemon tree, and mint, with its unmistakable fragrance, has taken over the yard as it does every spring. I'm happy to see my flourishing garden, eager to start weeding and get my hands in the dirt. And I'm happy to be with Charley, who also seems to be flourishing.

However, in Arizona, there is talk about hospice. When I check in with my brother after my return, he is frantic with anxiety. Mother won't use her walker. Time and again, he finds her struggling silently down the hall, using the walls to steady herself as she makes her way from the bedroom to the kitchen or the sunny living room.

Mother's doctor has informed her that she *must* use a walker. Mom is having none of it. She ignores or flatly refuses requests, reminders, or pleas. My brother, feeling responsible for her safety, is reduced to near panic.

As soon as I arrive in Arizona, I put in a call to the eldercare consultant my brother and I turn to when we need help. We certainly need it now. What can we do about a parent who is increasingly unable to care for herself but fighting fiercely to stay in control and maintain her independence?

Sherri, our consultant, agrees to come to the house the following day and provide the firmness that family members can't bear to assert. When she arrives, after greeting and chatting with our mom, she broaches the topic of the walker. "Your family loves you and wants you safe. Using a walker is about safety. If you fall, you might break your hip, and a broken hip can be fatal."

Mother's response is an emphatic, "No."

Sherri tells Mother gently that it's necessary to use the walker. "No!"

"In that case," Sherri explains, "it may be time to consider a living situation where professionals can keep you safe." Mother flat-footedly announces that she will *not* use the walker, and she will *not* consider assisted living. Still respectful, Sherri replies, "In a situation like this, others are obligated to keep you safe if you won't do it yourself."

"Well then, I'll commit suicide!" shrieks my mother in a total meltdown.

As I replay this scenario in my mind, I'm awed by the complexity of dealing with elders who have dementia. None of us anticipated what would happen next. Two weeks after I return home, I receive shocking news. Mother is faithfully using her walker. And she has stopped eating.

I hadn't counted on my mother's dementia progressing so fast. How dare I go away when she might need me. When I initially told Sherri my concerns about taking a sabbatical and being away for months at a time, she had been encouraging. "Your mother's condition could go on for years; you need to live your life." This was just the reassurance I needed. It was as if she'd handed me a passport filled with visas to all the places I hoped to go. I still check with Sherri each time I prepare to leave the country. This time, when I ask her, "Do you think it makes sense to go to Bali, or should I cancel my trip?" Sherri says, "Make your plans. But keep them tentative." And that's what I do.

———

When I return to Tucson two weeks later, I find my mother sweet and compliant . . . and nearly bedridden. I am shocked by how different she looks in just two weeks. She is visibly thinner, and her fingers and toes are icy. The household is tense with worry. None of us can make her eat.

We contact the hospice. "If things can be turned around, your mother will likely improve and have no need for hospice," says the visiting nurse. "If not, we can provide care during the final stage of her life."

"She kept her agreement," my husband points out when I call home. "She said if they forced her to use the walker, she'd commit suicide."

"How can we turn things around?" I ask Charley.

"Well, you can't un-ring the bell," he replies cryptically, "but perhaps you can ring a different bell." That bell, I realize immediately, will have to be one of tender love and appreciation, one that clearly acknowledges Mother's power and control.

So, for the next several days, I use every opportunity I can find. I lie next to my tiny mom, who looks even smaller under the pile of covers. I stroke her soft face and the inconceivably silky skin on the palms of her hands. I assure her that it gives me pleasure to come see her, although it hurts my heart to find her so uncomfortable. Each time she says, "Gosh, I can't remember a thing!" I remind her, "Mom, that's not true. You remember what matters most. You remember who you love and who loves you." That makes her smile.

When the moment feels right, I tell her how fortunate I feel to have had a mother all the way into my sixties. I am saying this to someone who lost her own mother when she was one week old, so I know this will be meaningful. Speaking softly, I tell her that I am going to miss her terribly when her life is over, and I hope she'll do everything in her power to stick around and let me enjoy having a mom for as long as possible.

The next day, Mother eats her breakfast and lunch and then asks for ice cream, her favorite food and an accurate barometer of her well-being. Her blood pressure returns to normal, and her fingers and feet warm up. Did my loving request make a difference? I'll never know. And besides, who cares?

By the end of my visit, I am exhausted but filled with hope. At least for now, it feels safe to go ahead with my journey.

———

It is early May. Charley is driving me to the San Francisco airport for my flight to Asia. Although I am sleepy, I am also excited. During my first week, I plan to attend a global healing conference in Bali. At the end of four months, I hope to meet and travel for two weeks with fellow members of a women's service choir. The time in between is waiting for discovery.

Late last night, in response to Charley's romantic overtures, I'd been perfunctory. "I am willing, but it's after midnight, so please be efficient."

"I'm really disappointed," he'd replied.

"I didn't say *no*; I just don't want to be romanced. I'm much more interested in sleep."

"Well, I'm really disappointed."

His tone had been far more accusatory than confiding. Both of us had tensed up. "Well, we could always bicker," I volunteered, "and then neither of us will get what we want. That's definitely an option."

We had made love—efficiently—and afterward, Charley sighed with contentment. "Ah, yes. We men are such simple creatures."

"No," I'd retorted. "A truly simple creature would say to himself, 'I want it. She doesn't, but she's willing. Lucky me; let's go for it!'"

We'd laughed, proud of ourselves for averting what could have been an hour of talk torture about what a turnoff my comment was, and how I had a perfect right to my feelings, and *blah, blah, blah*. Instead, we slept.

Now, full of nervous energy, I chatter as Charley drives toward the airport. He will drop me off and then hurry to his office to see patients. I look at my husband as he maneuvers the car through early-morning traffic. Charley is freshly shaved and looks handsome in his navy sport coat and blue-gray tie. His remaining mad-scientist flyaway hair is dark except for some white around the edges of his sideburns. While Charley is watching the road, I am watching him.

I think about the impact my trip is having on Charley. I remember how reluctant he was at the beginning, how long he'd postponed our discussion. What is it truly like for him? I know this man; he is my husband of nearly thirty years. And yet, in truth, he is not *my* anything. He is his own person with his own interests and concerns and feelings. To me, Charley is a comforting set of hands, an even voice, a steady, reassuring presence. But who is he to *himself*? What is it like to be that self?

"I wish I could spend a day inside your head," I muse aloud as we approach the Bay Bridge.

"Yes, you could get acquainted with a whole new set of insecurities," he retorts.

I laugh. Charley has always been smart, but only in recent years has this light and playful wit begun to emerge.

"I'm going to miss you," Charley remarks as we head down the peninsula toward the airport.

"So why are we doing this?"

"It wasn't my idea! I'm trying to help make your dream come true, remember?"

"Oh, right . . ."

We have arrived at the airport. At the drop-off curb, Charley and I share a long, sweet farewell kiss. He helps me shoulder my pack while I fasten the waist belt buckle and grasp the handle of my rolling carry-on. Turning toward the revolving entrance door, I feel a momentary clutch in my stomach. *Why do I keep going off on my own, throwing myself into situations that frighten me?*

The answers will come in their own sweet time.

CHAPTER 10

Did the Earth Move?

BALI

*H*ow quickly the adventure begins. My plane stops briefly in Taipei en route to Bali. In the women's restroom of the airport, I overhear two young women conversing with an older solo traveler. The girls plan to travel for four months all over Southeast Asia: Thailand, Cambodia, Laos, and Vietnam. "Be sure to go to India," advises the older woman. "And don't miss Varanasi; the funeral pyres on the Ganges are amazing."

I feel a stab of regret. I would love to visit each of those places. However, I know I won't be traveling like these young women. I will probably settle into life in one or two places and get to know them well. I wish I could do both, but I know what will make me happier.

From Taipei to Singapore and then on to Bali. I barely remember the shuttle ride to Ubud or falling into bed at my hotel. Ten hours later, I wake up with a groggy head, a stiff neck, and a scratchy throat. Peeking through the curtained windows of the hotel room, I see palm and pine trees and an inviting swimming pool below. I notice the balcony's elaborately carved mahogany rails in front of me and, above, the beautifully crafted upswept corners of the roof. I step outside. Hot! Seriously hot. I retreat into the room and return to my bed, where predictable thoughts arise right on schedule. *The swim season at home is just starting. The weather is perfect. Why did I leave my bicycle, my friends, and Charley?*

Stop it! I tell myself. *You're jet-lagged. You know transitions suck.* My sense of irony rescues me from feeling too sorry for myself. I envision travelers from previous centuries listening to me complain that it has taken thirty uncomfortable hours to get halfway around the world.

In the Amazon two years ago, Lynne Twist had mentioned a conference she would be attending in Bali: Quest for Global Healing. When I began planning my sabbatical, I decided this conference would provide a perfect introduction to Bali and a chance to meet others engaged in global activism.

So here I am. The Agung Rai Museum of Art is the venue for the conference that begins tomorrow. Today I have time to explore the grounds. I am grateful for the coolness of the forested park with its streams and bridges, lush plantings, and stone sculptures. If our initial hotel was lovely, our accommodations at the museum are opulent. I look over the thick conference program. It promises a feast of artistic extravaganzas: pageantry and gamelan music and Balinese dance. A heavy-hitting list of speakers has been invited. Among them are Desmond Tutu, the Minister of Labor and Human Resources for Bhutan, Indonesia's former president, and our own Lynne Twist.

I was anticipating a gentle introduction to Bali. However, plans don't always turn out as intended. There's nothing gentle about being surrounded by six hundred people; there is nothing gentle about five days of nonstop entertainment, speakers, workshops, and meals. As I rush around in the intense heat, I feel increasingly lonely and sad. Although the cultural pageantry is magnificent, the packed program and immense crowds actually *impede* connecting with the people of Bali and the other participants.

Little by little, my own modest efforts to make the world a better place feel puny and irrelevant. Sandwiched between my suitemate—the inspiring Lynne Twist—and Desmond Tutu, whose private villa faces our balcony, I feel like the child in that Jewish haiku: "Is one Nobel Prize so much to ask from a child, after all I've done?" I am quietly shriveling up with feelings of inadequacy. Although this isn't a very successful start to my Asian adventure, I console myself. *Think about it this way. You are only feeling worthless; at least you are not feeling scared.*

I do have one meaningful encounter. After a formal presentation by the Minister of Labour and Human Resources for Bhutan, I line up and speak briefly with him. Bhutan is the remarkable tiny nation whose Buddhist ruler is as interested in gross national happiness as he is in gross national product. I ask the minister if there are any English-speaking Buddhist teachers in Bhutan.

"Yes, there are a few," he affirms, "but most of them are traveling in the West." He continues, "Many Bhutanese are critical of them for leaving their country. I, however, think it is a good idea. Before they leave, I tell these teachers, 'Study well the suffering of people in the West, because as commerce and modern life come to Bhutan, it will soon become the suffering of the Bhutanese.'" For me, this conversation is far and away the most meaningful moment at the conference.

When the conference is over, I'm relieved. I move back to my original hotel. Charley will be arriving next week, and this is where we'll stay. Meanwhile, I wander up and down the shopping streets of Ubud, looking at clothing, jewelry, and an assortment of beautiful crafts. The conference organizers advised us to pack lightly and buy Balinese clothing when we arrived. In every way, my introduction to Bali is turning out to be a bad fit—literally. Day after day, I walk from my hotel into the center of Ubud, focusing on the sidewalks' missing grates to avoid falling into the open irrigation ditches beneath. Enervated by the heat and humidity, I *jalan-jalan* (stroll) along the shopping streets, entering little boutiques to try on clothing. Artful and affordable Balinese clothing is perfect for this climate, with cool, airy fabrics and light colors. I especially like the gauzy white eyelet blouses. However, all these clothes are sized for small-breasted women. Hot and sweaty, I cannot pull anything over my well-endowed chest. I keep looking; there must be *something* that fits. No luck.

One of the conference guests raved about the low-cost massages in Bali, so while I wait for Charley to arrive, I schedule some appointments at a little retreat nestled among the rice paddies in the cooler, nearby neighborhood of Penestanan.

Jassi is the English-speaking proprietor who spends time with her guests on the tree-shaded patio after their massages. One day, I watch her set out the morning offerings of rice and flowers and weave circles in the air with a stick of incense. I ask her, "What is in your mind and your heart as you make the offering?"

"Gratitude to the gods," Jassi responds. "You see, everything we need for our survival and happiness is already here: flowers for beauty and trees for wood, and bamboo and fruit . . . everything. We just give back a little of this as an offering to express our thanks."

While we sip our fragrant ginger tea, I explain that Western capitalism offers a very different cultural teaching. In order to maintain an ever-expanding economy, an artificial sense of need must be carefully cultivated. I tell her about writer Harold Kushner's wonderful observation that if one morning, every woman in America woke up completely satisfied with herself just as she was, the US economy would come to a grinding halt. Jassi's response is a warm, knowing laugh.

Before I leave, Jassi tells me that a wealthy man in Ubud has died and that there will be a cremation ceremony the following day. I am curious to see for myself Bali's renowned celebratory approach to death. Jassi directs me to the marketplace in Ubud where I must purchase a sarong and sash. These are required garb for attending Balinese ceremonies. In the morning, properly attired, I join a throng of men and women who are standing in the hot, hot sun waiting for the procession to begin. We watch family members putting final touches on an elaborately decorated papier-mâché tower and a platform holding a huge papier-mâché bull. Finally, after several sweaty hours in the sun, the dead man's grandson climbs up onto the bull. The crowd begins walking as the men of the *banjar* (small local communities) carry both floats—the tower and the bull—through the streets of Ubud. Accompanied by the sounds of gamelan and cymbals, the procession moves slowly toward the cemetery in the Monkey Forest.

When we arrive, crowds of people are milling around, chatting, and eating. The atmosphere is almost like a party. I am filled with curiosity as a man takes a knife and slices through the upper part of the bull. The top is lifted off and the corpse, wrapped in white cloth, is set inside the bull's body. Now, the lid is replaced. Women of the deceased man's family carry offerings; they circle the bull several times and then set their offerings beneath it. I'm riveted when men approach with torches. Soon the giant bull is in flames. As predicted, no one cries; there is no evidence of grief.

The woman who has just lost her mate appears completely tranquil while her husband's body is burning. I am puzzled. I know that the Balinese believe in reincarnation and that cremation is considered cause for celebration, since the spirit is now able to leave the body. But how can anyone transcend the bonds of human attachment and the loss of their beloved so quickly?

While wondering about the widow of the man who just died, I am also thinking about my mother. Whether her passing and my own grief are coming soon or not for a while, I know they are coming. My concerns about this inevitability fuel my curiosity.

The following day, I ask Jassi, "Do people in Bali *really* feel content at a cremation ceremony? What about having to give up being alive? What about missing the person you love?"

"Being alive is wonderful," she responds. "Of course, it is painful to lose loved ones. But our religion says, 'Don't cry. If you are sad, it will only make it harder for the spirit to leave.'"

"And what does the mother in you say?" I persist.

"The mother in me says I should hold the wife who is now a widow and tell her, 'It's OK to cry.' Hopefully, by the time of the creation ceremony, she will no longer need to cry."

Jassi's words reassure me. With all due respect to cultural differences and the need for sensitivity, I believe there are certain truths in the human heart and commonalities in the human condition that transcend geography and culture. I thank Jassi and tell her I'm grateful to have a friend and mentor here in Bali. Before I go back to my hotel, she teaches me a few phrases in Bahasa Indonesian: *tarima kasih* (thank you), *selamat pagi* (good morning), and *selamat siang* (good afternoon).

———

I have been in Bali for only two weeks when Charley arrives. I had asked him to visit toward the middle of my four months, when I would be settled in and more connected with people, but this was the only time he could fit into his work schedule. Still, I'm glad to welcome my adventuresome mate. Charley arranges for a guide. In my efforts to be frugal, I would never have considered this. Our guide takes us to visit craft villages, and afterward, we ride bicycles through the countryside. As we pedal along back roads, streams of excited children appear, shouting, "Hello, hello!" and gleefully slapping high-fives as we ride by.

When we reach a rice field where the plants are tall and golden, we stop to watch the harvesting process. Women wearing wide woven hats to protect their faces from the hot sun whack clumps of the long, just-harvested rice plants against an angled wooden panel. This vigorous process loosens the husk-encased kernels. The kernels fall to the ground at the base of the board; the rice plants are then tossed aside, and the women reach for another bundle. I take photos, and there are hoots of laughter as the women see their images on my digital camera screen. I most enjoy photographing an old, wrinkled crone with missing teeth, a wide-brimmed coolie hat, and an open face that has clearly weathered much . . . and endured. At the end of the workday, each woman will take home a large bag of rice. After the three-week harvest, her family will have enough rice to last until the next harvest.

Charley and I are intrigued by the communal nature of life in Bali. Even cremations have communal elements. "How do people who aren't wealthy afford a cremation ceremony?" I ask Jassi. She then describes what sounds like a "rent-a-crypt" program.

"Families who can't afford a cremation bury the body in a temporary grave while they save up money. Once they can afford it, they have the cremation, and some other family can use the burial plot." I'm startled and impressed; what a creative solution.

"Another way to make cremation more affordable," Jassi explains, "is group cremation." Later on, I'll see about twenty cremations taking place at once in a parklike setting with a festival atmosphere. Families bring picnics; there are food booths and balloons and kids playing games. With so many cremations taking place simultaneously, the smoke is overpowering.

But the *banjar* is by far the most communal aspect of Balinese life. The banjar is a community within a community. It consists of forty to fifty families. They share a temple, assist one another with chores, prepare for celebrations together, and help in the case of illness. Children play with same-age cousins; mothers and grandmothers prepare offerings and cook food together. Charley and I watch as groups of men construct and raise the ceremonial poles in preparation for the festival of Galungan. And the entire banjar assembles to prepare and carry out a cremation.

The banjar is no transient clustering of people. For generations, these families are bound together, providing support but also creating a set of social expectations from which one does not waver. An unruly adolescent, I will learn during my stay in Bali, would be confronted not just by his parents but by the elected leader of the banjar. If the boy would not heed the repeated warnings, the entire family might be asked to leave the banjar. Even the most defiant youngster would back down from such a consequence.

This way of life must sometimes feel constraining, but given how lonely I can feel, a banjar sounds like heaven on Earth.

———

After a few days, Charley and I fly to the huge neighboring island of Java. Java is a Muslim island. There is a mosque near our hotel, and I rapidly come to love the sound of the recorded chants that call the faithful to worship five times each day. Everywhere, women wear white scarves over their heads and necks. Muslim women in Java seem to be leading full and energetic lives. I am amused to see girls and women driving motor scooters with bright yellow helmets strapped over their traditional head coverings.

I've come to Java in search of batik. Yogyakarta and nearby Solo are the center of the batik textile industry. The wax-resist dye technique and the resulting fabric, with its distinctive patterns of dark blue paisley against the faintest blue background, or bold brown and gold against pale cream, have delighted me for as long as I can remember.

On our last day in Jogja, (the familiar name for Yogyakarta), we spend our afternoon visiting textile factories and shopping. When we return to our hotel laden with *batik* treasures, I set them out on a table. Tomorrow, we fly back to Bali together, and then Charley will leave early the following morning for San Francisco. I am already starting to miss him.

LEAH FISHER | 117

It is a shame to sleep in twin beds, but nothing else was available when we checked in. During the night, I wake around 5:00 a.m. to use the bathroom. Instead of returning to my own bed, I sit on the edge of Charley's and whisper, "Do you want company?" He slides over and lifts an arm to wrap around me. Lying on our sides, we quickly fall asleep in the narrow bed.

An hour later, our world starts rocking. It begins gently enough, but as the rocking becomes stronger and more persistent, I wake, realizing this is an earthquake. Because the initial rocking was so gentle and I was deeply asleep, it's hard to rouse myself. California earthquakes usually begin with a violent jolt that yanks me out of sleep, heart pounding in panic. Now I struggle to focus and remember where I am: Indonesia . . . Java . . . Yogyakarta.

The rolling motion has given way to shaking that grows progressively stronger and more violent. This quake is going on for a *very* long time. I can feel Charley's heart pounding against my back. Now I am fully alert, straining to remember anything I can about the building we're in. Our room is on the ground floor of a two-story hotel. I remember seeing heavy terra-cotta tiles on the roof. By now, the shaking has become violent. This is the longest earthquake I have *ever* experienced. It goes on and on. And on. I know there is a limit to what any building can withstand, and I believe we are approaching that limit. With calm, clear awareness, it sinks in: I am going to *die* in this bed— in Indonesia.

Buddhist teacher Jack Kornfield says, "We all know we are going to die. We just don't believe it." In that interminable sixty seconds, I believe it! Along with fear and anticipation of terror, I experience a cold, stunned surprise. *So, this is it. This is the end of my life . . . right now.* And then the shaking stops.

We hear voices outside our room, and Charley asks, "Don't you think it would be a good idea to go outside?" Hurriedly, fearfully, I grab the attractive loose-fitting batik dress I purchased yesterday; it is still neatly folded on the table next to an overturned floor lamp. Slipping it over my head, I turn to Charley. "If this is going to be my last day on Earth, I want to get some wear out of my new clothes." Charley laughs. We put on our sturdiest shoes and open the door.

Miraculously, our hotel seems intact. There are long cracks in the stucco walls and lots of overturned pots and planters. Afterward, Charley will tell me that while I was thinking we were about to die, he was calmly calculating the magnitude at about 6.2. He considered it a moderate earthquake. Although he will turn out to be correct about the Richter reading, I will be right in assuming we've just survived an earthquake that will claim many lives.

Outside the hotel, we find a crowd of people in the road. Everyone is looking around, stunned. Buildings and walls and small shops are totally flattened. We walk up and down our little street; the damage is overwhelming. Overhead lines have fallen into the road. The building directly across from the hotel is nothing but a pile of rubble. A child is crying; a woman sits on a low wall, her face in her hands. Down at the corner, furniture is being carried out of a multifamily building. Old people, young nursing mothers, babies, children, and pets are settling down on chairs and sofas right there in the road.

Although it is barely 7:00 a.m., and our flight to Bali doesn't leave until 2:00 p.m., Charley wisely suggests we pack and leave immediately for the airport.

A few minutes later, we are in a taxi making our way toward the airport. What would normally be a twenty-minute ride lasts several hours because throngs of people crowd the roadways. They are running in the streets, crying, and shouting. Families of five squeeze onto motor scooters, their faces looking strained and frightened. Car traffic is at a standstill. Pedestrians scramble onto the backs of pickup trucks. Once on board, they reach down to pull up relatives and strangers. A child, fearful of being left behind, begins to scream in terror.

Everyone seems to be running in the same direction. Charley and I don't understand why. Eventually, we realize these people are racing for higher elevation. Indonesians, still traumatized by the previous year's devastating tsunami, have gotten the idea that another tsunami is coming. Even though Yogyakarta is more than thirty kilometers from the sea, and despite announcements from policemen with bullhorns—"This is *not* a tsunami"— people are still desperate to get to higher ground. Ironically, their chosen destination is a huge overpass on the route to the airport. As Californians, Charley and I know that bridges and overpasses are the most dangerous places to be in an earthquake. The thousands of pedestrians, cycles, cars, and trucks clogging the overpass demonstrate something that Charley and I understand about post-traumatic stress. Instead of accurately assessing and responding to the disaster at hand, the crowd is reacting to a past trauma as if it were happening once again.

Our taxi driver uses skill, ingenuity, and determination to get us to the airport. Seeing the devastation along the way, I am reminded that income inequality isn't just about who gets a Mercedes and who gets a bicycle. It's also about who gets a rebar-reinforced home (or hotel) and who dies.

Almost two hours later, we arrive at the Yogyakarta airport. It has been shut down. The earthquake has damaged runways, so no planes can land or take off. Our taxi driver kindly offers to wait while we figure out how to get Charley back to Bali for his flight to the United States. Entering the terminal entrance, I notice a sculpture that has fallen through a plate glass window. The stone figure lies on its back surrounded by a halo of fractured glass.

If we can make it to the airport at Solo two hours away, we can fly to Jakarta and from there to Bali—hopefully arriving in time for Charley to make his flight home. Our taxi driver agrees to take us. Amid the chaos, he works calmly and diligently to get us to our destination. He intercedes with police and military personnel at closed roads. He backs us out of gridlocked highways.

We will later learn that the most severely damaged part of the city is precisely where our hotel was located.

On the long ride to Solo, I sit close to Charley in the back seat of the taxi. Leaning into him, I whisper, "The way you were holding me when the earthquake hit was perfect. If I've got to die, I can't imagine a better way to go than in your arms."

Charley looks over at me mischievously, and borrowing a line from Ernest Hemingway, he deadpans, "Oh, did the earth move for you too?"

CHAPTER 11

Picking up the Pieces

JAVA

*C*harley leaves Bali in the wee hours of the morning after kissing my breasts goodbye and whispering to each one separately how much he will miss it. Now it's once again time for me to leave our tourist accommodations and switch back to budget traveler mode.

I don't really want to be in Bali anymore. I feel drained and shaken. I'm sorely tempted to go home with Charley. But when I propose it, he objects. "I have a lot of work lined up, and I'd feel really jerked around if you came home early." My heart sinks. If marriage consists of you, me, and us, something is out of balance. Charley has a strong sense of "I" and a generous sense of "you." But his version of "us" can feel depriving and disappointing. If I were in a sturdier frame of mind, I'd be pissed off. Instead, I just feel bereft.

After Charley's departure in the morning, I walk to an internet café. I find emails from family and a few concerned friends who know geography and wonder if we might have been in Java. Our daughter, Shahla, is one of the first to email me. "I'm writing to make sure you weren't killed in an earthquake. I bet many people are terribly sad right now. Mom, have you started doing relief work yet? I know it's only been a few hours, but you *wanted* to find a project."

At a computer next to me, I notice a tall, attractive woman speaking with a male companion in American English. She is wearing a dramatic black, brown, and white beaded necklace. It's hard to take my eyes off her.

"Excuse me, I can't help staring. Your necklace is stunning."

"Thank you. I design jewelry and have the pieces made here in Bali." Janis and I introduce ourselves, and in a surprisingly short time, we discover that we're both Californians, both psychotherapists, and, remarkably, we both studied with the same beloved mentor.

I explain to Janis and her partner, Steven, that I survived yesterday's deadly earthquake in Yogyakarta. "My husband just left, and I'm looking for a place to live." They invite me to lunch, and over salads and Thai iced tea, Janis says, "I know a lovely couple with a guesthouse. If you'd like, we can go there and see if it's available."

By evening, I am happily situated in the village of Penestanan. For fifteen dollars a day, I am staying in a gorgeous two-story Balinese-style guesthouse. My hosts are a gentle, loving pair. Nyoman is a handsome young man in his mid-twenties. He works the night shift at a nearby hotel and speaks English. His wife, Kadek, is graceful and shy. She moves quietly and efficiently around the family compound, cleaning the guesthouse, caring for her child, and attending to the ceremonial rituals and domestic tasks of her home.

I have a new friend. Putu Lia is four years old, almost five. She has full black hair that poufs around an exquisitely delicate face. An only child, she is beautiful, well-mannered, and playful. She is obviously adored by her parents. Today, we are sitting side by side on the white cotton-and-wicker couch of my guest cottage, looking out at the gracefully curving terraces of the rice paddies. We are watching a group of young boys fly their kites and run along the narrow paths that edge the terraces. I am taking portrait photos of Putu Lia. Her steady gaze through soft brown eyes makes me want to drink in her face. She loves posing and makes me show her each picture on the digital screen before I may take another.

Each morning when I wake up in the king-size canopied bed, I begin my day with yoga, meditation, and journaling in the spacious room that comprises the entire upper floor of the guesthouse. It's a beautiful room with sliding glass walls. When the sliders are open, the room seems to extend beyond the decks through the cool morning air and into the rice paddies below. I watch a farmer working his field, alternately bending to tend his plants and standing to gaze at his crop. I imagine him patiently bearing witness to the slow, steady progress of the rice's development.

Putu Lia is restless. I can tell she wants me to finish writing in my journal so we can play. I give her a pen and paper to draw kites, balloons, and ABCs while I finish my writing. She is an exceptionally beautiful child in a country of exceptionally beautiful children.

I reflect on my happy landing after a rocky start in Bali. The insecurities that were stirred up by comparing myself with others at the conference have subsided. After being quite literally shaken up by the earthquake in Java, I finally feel anchored in Bali. As much as I enjoy Charley's company, both the conference and his visit confined me to a removed tourist role. Furthermore, my love for little Lia is starting to blossom.

I notice a pattern emerging. What consistently makes me happy is living with congenial families that have young children. I thrive on being part of a family . . . *without* having to be the mom! Even when I'm not engaged in a service project, these homestays provide a way to give back. Besides bringing income to host families, I see the effect on moms and dads when I play with their children or smile at their skillful parenting. Parenting is hard work. For me to witness and acknowledge their efforts and take delight in their children is a simple but meaningful gift. I feel like a global grandma.

Now I have a difficult decision to make. Before the earthquake I had planned on going to Amed, a remote fishing village on the northeast coast of the island. But how can I enjoy sitting on a beach knowing that people are suffering and grieving in Java? Should I go back to Yogyakarta to help? Of course I should. But I don't want to be there when Mount Merapi erupts. Or should I remain in my sweet rice paddy guesthouse? How long should I rest in the warmth of this cozy family before I venture back into the ring of fire? I go back and forth, my indecision tormenting me as it often does.

In the morning, I hear Putu Lia laughing and chattering in our shared courtyard. I know she is waiting for me. Yesterday, she shadowed me for most of the morning, playing catch with the inflatable globe, daintily sharing fruit salad from my plate, proudly singing "Happy Birthday" in English. By now, we are creating a morning ritual. When I finish yoga and meditation, I go out on my balcony and call, "Putu Lia . . . Putu Liiiia." She promptly and excitedly calls back, "Mama Leah, Mama Leeeeah!" Then I come downstairs, and we play.

My kind friend Janis stops by. We sit on the stoop of Nyoman and Kadek's small house, and I explain my dilemma. Janis's reaction is, "It's OK to move back and forth between self-nurturing and service. You were clearly in shock when I met you. I think you need to come back to *yourself* before you return to help others. You'll know when it's time."

Without a doubt, meeting Janis and Steven is the turning point in my Bali adventure. Like a fairy godmother, a kind woman appears out of nowhere right after an earthquake has shaken me to my core. She stays for only three days, but during that time, she takes me under her wing, reminds me that I can trust myself, and leads me to a home, a family, and a child who shares my name.

Each morning when I open my front door, Kadek brings me a hot cup of coffee. Putu Lia is with her. Soon we start our daily game of Bali Ball. Nyoman is the only English speaker in this family. It's easy to forget that Lia and I don't share a common language. The child is so bright and attentive that we have no trouble understanding each other. Putu Lia and I use the inflatable globe for playing catch and geography lessons. She has quickly learned to find San Francisco, Bali, and Australia. Now I'm showing her Canada and Africa.

Janis was right in predicting I'd know when I was ready to return to Jogja. After six peaceful days with gentle Kadek, handsome Nyoman, and playful Lia, I think the time has come. I am beginning to feel restless, a sign that I must be ready to volunteer my help. However, volunteering is not so easily arranged. I spend two days trying to reach the Red Cross, USAID, and multiple other relief organizations. Emails go unanswered; no one returns my phone calls. It is maddening. Time is passing; the need is huge; I have the necessary skills. I am stumped until I remember a childhood friend who now works in the diplomatic service of the US State Department. I email her, explaining I'm in Bali and eager to be of service in the aftermath of the Java earthquake. Thanks to her help, within hours, I hear from someone in the State Department with a contact name and Yogyakarta phone number. Hurray for the young girl network!

———

My flight to Yogyakarta is about to arrive. Above the clouds, I can see the peaks of five mountains. The smoking one must be Mount Merapi. However, the smoke that was white just a week ago is now a horrible gray black. *Am I crazy to return? God was gracious enough to spare my life once; why press my luck? Please, Mother Nature, be still for a little while.*

The hotel in which Charley and I survived the earthquake is closed due to structural damage, but a staff member recommends another hotel a few blocks away. As I pull my suitcase around the block, I am aghast. The entire area looks like it was bombed. Piles of rubble line the sidewalks in front of every building. Now piled neatly, they look like enormous berms of stone stretching up and down the street. Half of all the buildings in Yogyakarta were damaged. And so many people are dead. Already, six thousand deaths have been confirmed.

Everywhere in the neighborhood, people are camped outside their homes under large blue plastic tarps. Their indoor life continues, just relocated outside their front doors. I pass families cooking over fires, watching TVs, sitting on sofas, and sleeping on mattresses. Beautiful batik fabrics form flimsy privacy curtains around the sleeping areas. Life goes on in these tarp towns. I marvel at how readily humans can adapt to their circumstances.

The following day, I follow up on leads from my State Department contact. I spend a full day making my way around the shattered city to meet with the director of Disaster Operations for the Red Cross. When I tell him I am trained in disaster mental health, and I can provide my own translator, he approves my request, assigning me to a Red Cross psychosocial team serving the hard-hit community of Klaten.

I met Jenny back on the tarmac at the Bali airport. We were both waiting to see if we could board a military transport to Java. Jenny could. As a foreigner, I couldn't. Jenny already had a volunteer assignment. I didn't. This lively, outgoing young woman is trilingual, speaking English, Bahasa Indonesian (the unifying national language), and the Javanese dialect. Yesterday, she emailed to say she dislikes her volunteer assignment and wants to team up with me as a translator.

A long-ago friend in the State Department and a translator

who dislikes her assignment. Without this serendipity, I would still be wandering the streets of Yogyakarta, frustrated and lonely.

I begin my assignment with a mixture of delight and terror. Our team leader, Amin, is waiting for Jenny and me at the Red Cross and Red Crescent office in Klaten. I'd expected to meet an elderly Indonesian man, but Amin turns out to be twenty-seven years old, a delightful beanpole of a young man from India. Despite his youth, Amin is a fine team leader: warm, courteous, and helpful. Like Putu Lia, Amin respectfully addresses me as "Mama Leah." After he introduces me to the psychosocial team, we pile into a Red Cross minivan and depart for three villages outside of Klaten, where rebuilding is going on. Volunteers are clearing debris, setting up water systems, and pumping out sewage.

In one of the villages, with Amin's help, I ask a group of children how they are doing and how they are feeling. "Fine," says one boy. How are they sleeping and eating? "Fine." I persist. A small girl replies that she wants her house back and that she misses her grandpa, who died in the earthquake.

"What helps when you're feeling sad?" I ask her.

"Hugs from my grandma."

Looking around at the devastation, I can imagine that a lot of hugs are going to be needed for a very long time.

Although it took perseverance, I am exactly where I need to be. I have a role in a meaningful project, and I'm getting to work closely with a dedicated group of young people. Still, it's complicated. Klaten sits immediately south of Mount Merapi. Part of the southern face of the mountain has already collapsed, and the volcano is expected to erupt within the next two weeks. I am scared.

The Red Cross is providing our housing, but Jenny and I can't stay with the main group because their hotel is full. Our accommodation feels like a ghost hotel. It is poorly managed and appears even more poorly built. There is no front desk and no housekeeping service. During our two-week stay, no one cleans the room. We are without toilet paper, soap, and potable water.

Rooming with Jenny is a unique experience. We enjoy companionable moments, like when she surreptitiously photographs me in my underwear brushing my teeth with Diet Coke.

There are also irritating moments. Our hotel room has just one bed, so Jenny and I are not only roommates but bedmates. I get used to sharing a bed, but sharing Jenny's nightly phone calls is more difficult. At 2:00 a.m., I hear her cell phone ring followed by an hour of loud whispering and laughing under the covers as she talks with her boyfriend. Eventually, I learn to sleep through it.

Sharing a bed with Charley is very different. When I think about our bed at home, I start to imagine Charley being attracted to some other women. So far, he has been content with fantasies. I wonder if it will stay that way.

Day and night, strong aftershocks set my heart pounding. The expanding cracks in the walls of our hotel fuel my anxiety. Anything that hasn't already fallen down looks like it's about to. I greet each morning with relief. While people are resuming their lives—riding scooters, running hotels, burying the dead, and sifting through the rubble for materials with which to rebuild their homes—we all know the earth below us is lurching with energy, and the mountain beside us is ready to explode with fire.

Several days into my volunteer service, the driver of our Red Cross van opens Jenny's door when I'm not looking. The slight rocking of the vehicle triggers a sudden jolt of terror. I realize that along with being a disaster volunteer, I'm also a fellow earthquake survivor.

At night, in our hotel room with only a dim hanging light bulb for illumination, Jenny and I prepare a training session for teachers faced with helping traumatized schoolchildren. In another community, we will facilitate a women's support circle. Meanwhile, the psychosocial team organizes daily activities for children whose schools are too damaged for them to enter.

It is my first experience working side by side with followers of the Muslim faith. All the female Red Crescent workers and the schoolchildren wear white head coverings. At first, I observe them with curiosity. Very quickly, the sense of strangeness wears off, and I take pleasure in the tiny, delicate head coverings on the little girls, the call of the muezzin, and the quiet departures of team members for prayer several times a day.

When we visit the village of Birin, people are busily clearing rubble from collapsed houses, tearing down dangerous structures, and making neat piles of reusable brick. Construction has already begun. Scaffolding surrounds a partially damaged house. Three men, sweating from the humidity, reach down to grab the bricks being handed up to them. As I watch, I feel frustrated and sad. I know the need to rebuild is urgent, but nobody in these villages can afford the rebar needed to stabilize the walls. Although international aid is flowing in, funds are not yet available. These laboriously rebuilt houses will be as vulnerable to earthquakes as the ones that have just collapsed.

Our psychosocial team is tasked with providing recreational activities and creating a safe place for the children to laugh and be happy for a few hours. Today, handsome Leo is leading a circle dance. It is something about a chicken and a duck: "*Ayam-be-beck*." As he does his crazy antics, with twitching buttocks and flapping arms and a lot of peck-peck-pecking, the children explode with laughter.

While the children are playing, a teammate calls Jenny and me over to a cluster of women and children. He asks me to speak with a mother whose five-year-old son was killed when the wall of their house collapsed on him. The grieving mother wants to know what she can do to get rid of her sadness. Jenny translates. I ask the young woman if she can sleep and eat. She has difficulty sleeping. She has no interest in eating, but she has been able to cook for her family and take care of them.

We are sitting outdoors on a log bench: Jenny, the mother, and I. Neighbors, friends, and other volunteers are milling about and discreetly listening to our conversation. Mothers are bathing young children in an outdoor tub. As we talk, wriggling wet bodies wrapped in towels are carried past us. With Jenny's assistance, I question the distressed mother. I explain to my young interpreter that I want to distinguish whether this woman is feeling bad in the sense of feeling badly, or whether she might also be feeling guilty. "Does she feel that she herself is bad?"

Jenny shoots me a look that says, *What are you talking about?* "That's ridiculous," she protests. "It was an earthquake!"

"Please ask her anyway." Reluctantly, Jenny translates my question.

"Yes!" the mother replies, looking obviously relieved. "I feel like such a bad mother! I feel I should have been able to protect him."

With Jenny's help, I explain to the grieving mother that her sadness and feeling bad is a normal response to losing her precious child. "You can't avoid feeling overcome with sadness. It is to your credit that you can still cook and care for your family. But when you start feeling that *you* are bad, there *is* something you can do." The woman looks at me with curiosity. "Mothers are very powerful—we all know that. We give birth to human life! We feed our babies out of our own bodies and watch them grow stronger. We comfort them, and they stop crying. But powerful as we mothers may be, we are *not* more powerful than an earthquake." I pause to let this sink in. "Every time you start to think that you were a bad mother, I suggest you stop and remind yourself that you are not more powerful than an earthquake. You will still be very, very sad. But I don't think you will feel so much like you are a bad person or a bad mother."

The mother listens carefully to Jenny's translation. There is a long pause while the three of us sit quietly. "Tell her she is wise," the woman instructs Jenny. "I will try what she suggests."

In the village of Birin, a group of mothers sit in a circle. Our morning's conversation is a chance for them to exchange ideas for helping their children deal with the disaster. Jenny translates my welcome. "Let's describe our *own* experiences of the earthquake before talking about what our children need and how we can help them." The stories they tell, much like those of the women in the *albergue* in Guatemala, are of unbearable loss, persistent fear, and, for some, utter despair. "In just one minute, the earthquake destroyed everything I spent a lifetime building," says one elderly woman. "I don't have enough years left to build it all again."

"Our children are afraid it will happen again," reports one mother. Every time the ground shakes, they get scared and cry."

"It's not just the children," says another participant. "It makes us afraid too. It happens all day long." I invite the women to think of three things they can do to comfort their children. "Talk, listen, and give hugs" is what they come up with.

I want to end this gathering on a hopeful note, so I steer the discussion to the special contributions of women. I remind them that they possess important skills needed for healing their trauma-tized community. "We women gather in groups; we talk; we hug; we express our feelings; we keep going even when we don't feel like it. While the men are clearing away the rubble and rebuilding the houses, we are rebuilding our families and our community in other important ways." As Jenny translates, I see many in the group look at one another and nod their heads in agreement.

When the meeting is over, Jenny continues to talk anima-tedly with the women. They listen attentively. I ask one of our team members what she is saying, and he explains that she's giving the women advice.

"Oh, what is her advice?" I ask with curiosity.

With a grin, he explains. "She's telling them, 'Don't sign any-thing. If the government wants you to sign something, don't do it. If you wait, you'll probably get more money.'"

I'm not sure how the Red Cross would feel about this advice, but it's been valuable to have a translator, and by now it's perfectly clear that Jenny is not a follower.

———

Before the earthquake, Charley and I had visited an art school in Yogyakarta. Now that I am volunteering, I realize that a disaster workbook might benefit the children here in Java.

I somehow find my way back to the school, and I commission a series of ten drawings for a coloring book that portray the earthquake: buildings damaged, children being reunited with families, rebuilding efforts, and the return to normalcy. Unlike in my protracted experience in Guatemala, these drawings are ready in two days. However, there is a problem: I am flying back to Bali tomorrow.

Just hours after the beautifully rendered drawings are delivered, I run into an energetic American social worker I've met while volunteering. Laine lives in Indonesia and has been doing disaster relief. I show her the new coloring book drawings and describe the workbook I produced in Guatemala. I explain that these drawings are the first step toward a similar effort in Java. But since I'm leaving in the morning, I need to find someone to take over this project. The social worker tells me she has a contract with the Australian government to help Indonesian children and families. I am elated when she says yes, she'll take charge of completing the project.

Nine months later, a booklet with a sleek illustrated yellow cover will arrive in the mail. The text is in Bahasa Indonesian, and the familiar drawings on the coloring pages are beautifully reproduced. Laine has included a note explaining that Australian funding made it possible to print and distribute thousands of these booklets to children affected by the earthquake.

I call to thank her. "I've been wondering how you've used the booklets."

"I trained kindergarten and preschool teachers to use them with the children." I am completely taken by surprise. I ask her why.

"Many children got separated from their parents during the earthquake. The youngest ones couldn't say where they lived. They didn't know their full names or their parents' names beyond *Ibu*, Mommy, and *Bapak*, Daddy. For this reason, some of the children were never reunited with their parents."

I wince with pain, visualizing a child yearning for their parents while the grieving parents assume their child is dead. When I think back to the day of the earthquake, it's not hard to believe that with so many deaths and so much chaos, young children who got separated from parents might never find them. Laine's choice to direct our booklet to this population is inspiring.

This joint enterprise teaches me something unforgettable and wonderful about international volunteer work. Sometimes, when you birth a project, other hands guide it forward, and eventually, it can end up helping where you least expect it!

CHAPTER 12

Meeting My Grandmother in Bali

BALI

I walk into the peaceful compound at Ubud Bodyworks and sit in the shady garden courtyard. I am waiting for the man whose picture is on the card I am holding. The day before Janis left for California, she handed me this card. "His name is Ketut Arsana, and he is an amazing healer. That earthquake is still inside you. I think he could be helpful."

Now, as I wait on the comfortable garden bench, grateful for a reprieve from the sweltering heat, I anticipate my meeting with Ketut. I have no idea what to expect. Will we just talk, or will the session be hands-on? Will I undress or stay clothed? Will he use trance work? Truthfully, it doesn't matter. It can't possibly be more arduous than taking ayahuasca in the Amazon or more bizarre than our shamanic cleansing in Otavalo. I am ready to experience whatever Balinese healing has to offer, no matter how unfamiliar or improbable.

In Bali, it is thought that psychological difficulties stem from a disturbed relationship with the ancestors. Healing comes about by reconnecting with the ancestors and repairing the problem in the relationship. Such beliefs may seem difficult for Western practitioners to understand. I find them foreign yet fascinating. I know I am in need of healing, and I am wide open.

After a while, a brown berry of a man with warm, twinkling eyes and a long white beard that belies his wrinkle-free face comes out and welcomes me. I follow him up a winding outside staircase to what seems like the very rooftop of Ubud. Ketut's treatment room looks out over a breathtaking vista of temples and rice paddies. I see a flock of white herons flying above the lush canopy of tropical trees.

Once inside his treatment room, I tell Ketut that I recently survived the Java earthquake.

"You were very lucky."

"Yes, but I've always struggled with a fear of death. I am so afraid that it interferes with my enjoyment of being alive."

"That's because you fight it," Ketut responds immediately. "You just need to surrender. After all, this body is not yours. You must return it to the Mother."

"I know that with my mind but not here." I touch my chest and belly.

"*I* am not afraid of death," the healer volunteers. "I have wanted to die at different times ever since I was eight years old." My immediate thought is that Ketut's mother must have died during his childhood. For an eight-year-old to flirt with death, he must be well acquainted with traumatic loss.

Indicating that I should lie down on his treatment table, Ketut begins a systematic exploration of my body. It is part massage, part acupressure, and part chiropractic adjustment. Ketut applies an extreme pressure that comes just to the edge of being too painful, and then he releases it. How does he know?

As his hands explore my fully clothed body, I ask him, "Did your mother die when you were a child?"

"Yes, my mother, and soon after, my grandfather, and then my older brother."

As he continues to press and probe, I tell Ketut that my mother's mother died just days after giving birth to my mother, and that her father died two and a half years later. "I feel like I carry her fear inside me."

"Yes, her spirit is connected to you."

"Oh, she is not dead."

"Her spirit is trying to connect with you," he repeats with quiet conviction.

"She's ninety-two years old, but she is still alive," I explain once again. Perhaps he doesn't understand what I'm saying. Ketut's spoken English is excellent, but maybe his comprehension isn't as good.

All the while, Ketut's hands are moving, pressing here, stretching there. "Not your mother," he clarifies. "*Her* mother."

Oh! I am taken aback. Stunned. Whatever Ketut is doing has a calming effect. I am no longer resisting the pressure of his hands. I gather my thoughts. "She was only twenty-nine when she died."

This is the story I have heard all my life, told without much detail—just a few facts, not really a story at all. How my mother's mother died in childbirth. How in the days before antibiotics, she died of infection, leaving my mother a motherless child.

The actual story is everything that is missing. Who attended my grandmother during those ten days? Was she at home or in a hospital? What was it like for my young grandfather? Who cared for the newborn and her six-year-old sister? Who cared for her in the months and years after her mother's death? Was it one person, a hired helper, or a fleet of relatives? Did the infant who was my mother come to know one reassuring pair of hands, one comforting scent--or were the hands and the scent frequently changing?

After a pause, I ask, "Do you suppose she knew she was dying?"

"Yes, I think so."

Suddenly, I am shivering. Of course! Of course she would fight death. She would be devastated and perhaps terrified. She would want desperately to live, to take care of her beloved six-year-old daughter and her newborn baby girl. My chest begins to expand with a huge heartful of sadness. *Imagine the pain of knowing you are dying and you can't prevent it. Imagine feeling utterly responsible for these little ones, yet unable to stay alive to protect them. Of course you would fight your death!*

As I experience the immensity of this sadness inside me, Ketut touches the place on my forehead known as the third eye, then my heart, and then my belly, ever so lightly. I feel perfectly held. I start crying softly, soundlessly.

In that moment, I understand the vast difference between dying after a fulfilling life, with children launched and important dreams realized, and dying at twenty-nine with two young children, one a newborn. For me, the prospect of death has always provoked pervasive, overwhelming fear. Now, in a flash of deep recognition, I see that there is dying, and there is dying. No matter what the circumstances, the letting-go involved in dying is probably hard and scary and sad. Yet there is something understandable about dying after progressing through all of life's seasons. Dying just after giving birth to a vulnerable new life must feel unbearable.

"What was your grandmother's name?" Ketut asks me.

"I don't know. My mother's adoptive parents preferred not to discuss it, and my mother was careful never to ask. Her older sister, who was adopted by a different family, might have told me once, but I've long since forgotten. And my mother can't remember; I've asked her."

"Go home tonight and make an offering to her. Make an offering to your grandmother, and she will come to you."

Back in my room in the guest bungalow, I set up an altar on a low table. I look around for offerings. I place flowers on it: fragrant frangipani from a vase near my bed. I put my bra on the altar . . . to honor the breasts that might have fed my mother had my grandmother lived. I also place on the altar a tiny purple-and-black beaded pouch that Putu Lia's mother, Kadek, made for me. I write a note to my forgotten grandmother. I tell her that her baby girl has lived a long and satisfying life, that she enjoyed an extremely happy marriage and had children who had children who now dream of having children. I fold the note, making it small enough to fit into the little pouch. I slip the beaded button through the loop to close it and place the pouch on my altar.

At two in the morning, I wake up, fully alert. Suddenly I know her name: Clara! I am almost certain of it. Now I speak to her by name: "Grandmother Clara."

I lie awake in my comfortable bed with its canopy and delicate, dotted sheer mosquito netting. A firefly has gotten into the bedroom and flits above the canopy. It is like having a personal visit from Tinkerbell. In my mind, I hear her say: "If you believe in fairies, clap your hands." And I can imagine her saying, "If you believe in spirits, make an offering, and create an altar and write a note to your grandmother and slip it into a beautiful, beaded pouch. Even if you *don't* believe in spirits, do it anyway. Speak to your grandmother by name. Tell Clara that you understand what agony it must have been for her to know she was dying and leaving a six-year-old and a newborn to fend without a mother. Tell her that you will honor her memory, tell your own children about her, and always be grateful for the gift of your mother."

Later, when I return home to Charley and talk about my healing with Ketut, he isn't as surprised as I expect. He has been following research in the field of epigenetics. He explains that recent studies suggest the impact of trauma isn't always a result of direct personal experience but can be passed on from a traumatized individual to future generations. The science is super complex, but the takeaway is that a vulnerability to symptoms of trauma can derive from ancestors we've never met.

My mother's trauma expressed itself as a fear of losing anyone she deeply loved. The essence of my fears, like that of my grandmother's, is primarily about having to die. By directing my attention one generation further back, Ketut helped me validate something I've sensed intuitively. My dread of death did not begin with me, nor does it totally belong to me.

So, thanks to an earthquake in Java and a healer in Bali, I retrieved a rejected part of my family history, a part that was disowned almost like a dirty secret. How strange to travel halfway around the world to meet my grandmother and welcome her back to her rightful place in my family.

I am glad to have found my grandmother Clara. I will remember her and honor her short life. But I don't need to feel her feelings as if they were mine—especially that helpless terror about having to die. By acknowledging the inherited part of my obsession with death, perhaps my encounter with Ketut will not only help me but possibly benefit future generations. I can hold Clara in my heart without having to *be* her. I want to be myself: my own inquisitive, quirky self, grateful for a long life and eager to keep exploring the world.

CHAPTER 13

The Space Between the Notes

BALI

*N*ow I feel like I've earned the right to some peaceful time on a warm beach. I am ready for swimming, snorkeling, and solitude.

My destination is Amed, a small, out-of-the-way fishing village. I arrive at Three Brothers Bungalows, which has six inexpensive oceanfront cottages. Rolling my carry-on bag through the gate, I discover a long chain-link fence down the middle of the property. It appears that even in paradise, brothers can have fallings-out.

In the morning, I wake up in a light, bright cottage so new that it still smells of freshly cut wood. I put on a swimsuit, gather my snorkel gear, and emerge from the bungalow to a glorious day. The sun is caressing; the ocean directly in front of my cottage is inviting. I eagerly accept the invitation, slip on my fins, and swim straight out from shore. Almost immediately, I see an abundance of blue starfish. They are a soft Wedgwood color with hints of violet, precisely like the irises blooming in my garden at home. Not fifteen yards out from the pebbly shore, I discover corals: huge cabbages tinged with lime-green edges. Beneath my fins swim tiny sapphire-blue fish. The contrast of electric blue against the sunlit chartreuse coral is psychedelic. It's like swimming in a stoner's lava lamp. I couldn't be happier.

"Hey, Leah!" I lift my head and look around. Three preteen girls I met yesterday afternoon sit on the low rock wall that separates my bungalow from the water. "Sing us a song," they command.

I emerge from the sea, rinse off at the convenient outdoor shower, and settle down to play. These girls and some younger children accost the guests, begging us to buy their necklaces: long single strands of tiny seed beads. Some people say no. Others buy a strand, only to have a dozen more children mob them, pleading, "Buy from me! Buy from me!" After observing this routine a few times, I inform the children who approach me: "If you do not ask me again, not even *once*, I will buy a necklace from every one of you on my last day in Amed." So now, they question me, "Is this your last day? How many more days till your last day?" I tell them, and we settle down to play. We sing songs in English: "The Itsy Bitsy Spider," "John Jacob Jingleheimer Schmidt," and the only Balinese song I know: "Di Sini Senang, Di Sana Senang." Onlookers smile at the three eleven-year-old Balinese girls and the sixty-something American singing together.

Three Brothers Bungalows has an informal outdoor restaurant right at the water's edge, and toward evening, guests appear. Almost all are from Holland. This makes sense when I remember that Indonesia was formerly a Dutch colony. I notice two women in their thirties. They look interesting, and I ask if I may join them for dinner. I've made a good choice. A sturdy and hilarious Dutch couple, they are in Bali for their honeymoon. We relish our meal, a perfect pairing of freshly caught grilled barracuda, several Bintang beers apiece, and a large serving of laughter. Afterward, our young Balinese waiter brings out a guitar, and soon we are having an impromptu sing-along. "Stand by Me,"

"Stairway to Heaven," "Country Roads." No matter that the guitar is hopelessly out of tune. There are some grimaces at the worst notes, but mostly we are all exuberant.

During my stay, I snorkel each day among the throngs of tiny angelfish and baby parrotfish. Babies of all species are adorable, and these tropical fish are no exception. How peaceful I feel. Floating on my back and looking up toward shore, I can see clouds surrounding Mount Agung like a fluffy shawl. The sun on the sea makes dancing sparkles of light. Coconut palms separate the seascape from the mist-filled valleys and lush hills that comprise the interior of the island.

I usually enjoy a second swim in the late afternoon as the sun goes down. The tropical fish and superb coral are still visible at dusk. But now, in addition, the fishing boats are coming back. These spiderlike catamarans have colorful sails that resemble the webbing in giant ducks' feet. One of them crosses my path as a solitary skipper guides it back to the little harbor. Gentle waves urge me toward shore. If I don't resist by swimming back out, I will eventually wash up on the black pebbles of the beach. Chances are, a few of the younger boys competing with the girls for my attention will find my sandals and gallantly bring them to the water's edge.

The people who run Three Brothers are warm and friendly. I especially like an outgoing woman who, like Putu Lia's mother, is named Kadek. She speaks perfect English. One morning, after bringing breakfast on a tray to the porch of my bungalow, Kadek offers to take me to see her home if I'm interested. Of course I'm interested. I climb on the back of her scooter, and we ride inland—where the Balinese live. Kadek introduces me to her husband. He is one of the "Three Brothers." They and their children live in a compound with several other households. Kadek brings out homemade lemonade, a welcome antidote to the intense heat. We all relax on the front stoop of her house, drink the lemonade, and chat.

It is a privilege to be invited to someone's home. Visiting Kadek's compound is a chance to learn more about her and this spiritually focused country. When I find an opening, I explain to Kadek that in America, we have so many choices it can be hard to identify a purpose or know if we are fulfilling it. "I wonder how Balinese people find their purpose in life?"

"We do ceremony; we go to the temple and we pray to God," she responds.

"What do you ask God?"

"Please send more tourists to Bali. Please make business good. Please bring money."

I like this candid, petite woman. Her approach to prayer is certainly different from my own, but I am eager to know more. "What would you say is most important to you and other Balinese people?"

"What's important to us is family," Kadek continues. "We all live together and help each other." Having said this, she gets up and excuses herself. I watch with curiosity as she enters a house across the path and returns holding a small baby. A young woman I assume is the child's mother follows close behind.

"This baby isn't growing properly," Kadek explains to me. "She doesn't want to eat, and she is sad and crying all day long. She is such an unhappy child."

The child takes one look at me and begins to shriek. "She thinks you are a doctor." Kadek hands the baby back to the mother, who attempts to nurse her. Although the child is eighteen months old, she doesn't appear to be more than seven months.

"You are a health professional," says Kadek. "What do you think is wrong with her?" I am amused by her easy leap from mental health counselor to medical care provider. But I ask enough questions to learn that the young parents are attentive and loving.

"Perhaps the baby needs to be evaluated by a doctor."

"They've already taken her to our healer. He gave medicine, but the child did not improve. And now the mother is growing discouraged and depressed."

Sitting in the warm sun, sipping my cool lemonade, I think about this baby. No wonder her young mother feels depressed. Imagine nursing one's baby all day long with nothing to show for it but an underweight, wailing child. Watching them, I remember the researcher from the Centers for Disease Control that Charley and I met in Guatemala. He told us that chronic parasites and bacterial infections can impair growth at a crucial time in a child's development and have lifelong consequences.

"I think this child needs a special doctor with a laboratory. The doctor can do tests that show exactly what is making the baby sick and what medicine will make her better."

Kadek shakes her head. "The family can't afford it. They would have to travel to the capital and pay a lot of money for that kind of doctor."

"How much would it cost?"

"About thirty dollars," says Kadek.

"If I gave them this money, would they use it to take the baby to the doctor?"

"Yes, I can assure you. They are so concerned about their child. They would definitely use the money to help her."

Back at Three Brothers, I give Kadek thirty dollars. I can't help wondering if I'm being played and reeled in like one of those beautiful fish. But I comfort myself that there are worse ways to be taken in.

I have a chance to learn more about Kadek the next morning when I investigate the dive shop just across the road. Chatting with the friendly Dutch owner, I mention visiting Kadek's home and my encounter with the failure-to-thrive baby. I ask if she has manipulated me or if she has enlisted me in a worthy cause. "Yes and yes" is his assessment.

"Kadek is definitely a businesswoman, and she is also quite

astute. It's true that there is no money in Bali for specialists. If someone has an eye problem or needs a cesarean, the family may have to sell a cow or some land. So, if she sees that you love children and have money, she might ask you to help this child." After the dive shop owner's reassurance, I feel better and put the incident out of my mind.

The following day, I wake to another sparkling morning. When I put on my fins and snorkel mask, I am alone in the water except for one other woman. I notice her again as I return from a spectacular swim among the tropical fish and coral. She is standing in the water just past the gently breaking waves. We introduce ourselves. Her name is Samantha, and she looks to be around fifty. She is American, although she currently lives in Australia. Surprisingly quickly, she begins telling me about the handsome young Balinese man who has been riding up to her bungalow on his motorcycle every night, much to the curiosity of the other guests. She explains that several years ago, she befriended and then fell in love with this man, who is twenty-five years her junior. She comes back and forth to Bali as often as she can. A few months ago, she found out that her lover has had a baby with a young Balinese woman. Samantha was devastated. Utterly devastated.

"I am just so angry I don't know what to do."

Out of the peacefulness of the morning, the gentle waves, and my relaxation comes a decades-old memory. I ask Samantha if I can share a story with her. She agrees.

"I've known this couple since we were all in our twenties. They married young, and he went on to become a minister. I really admire them. They've always had a loving, respectful relationship and share a commitment to live in a generous, authentic, and caring way. Even so, after they'd been married quite a few years—I think their children were teenagers by then—the minister came to his wife very upset and told her he'd been having an affair. Furthermore, the woman was pregnant with his child. I know nothing about my friend's initial reaction, but here's what I do know. She was not going to live with secrecy or shame. In keeping with their deepest values, she decided that if this is her husband's baby girl, then she is family. Both the child and her mother are included in birthdays, holidays, and special events. That child has three caring adults in her life; she has half brothers and sisters, and she has grown up with absolutely no sense of shame about herself."

Samantha looks surprised, and then her face relaxes. "I think *I* might want to do that. Up until now, I've just wanted to punish and hate him."

"Have you had enough of punishing and hating him? These things can't be hurried."

"Oh, I've hated him plenty! I really have. And all the while, he has been so steadfast. Did I mention . . . he named the baby Samantha? He stays devoted to me, he's devoted to the mother, and he's totally involved with his little daughter. He is really a most unusual man."

When Samantha gets out of the water, I put on my snorkel again and swim back toward the coral, content to have shared this remarkable story. Perhaps the timing is just right, and it will show Samantha another possibility. Perhaps the courage and integrity of my long-ago friends will take root in another family on the opposite side of the world. Then again, maybe my conversation with Samantha will be just a passing moment that floats out on the next tide. As I flutter my fins carefully over the delicate coral, I remind myself to remain pure of heart about the outcome. I have shared the story; what comes of it is not up to me.

Evening comes, and after another spectacular sunset, the rollicking Dutch honeymooners and I spend a magical evening sitting around the restaurant singing, accompanied by bongos, a tambourine, and the same out-of-tune guitar. A German man finally tunes the waiter's guitar, to the immense gratitude of all the guests. I'm taking photos when the baby daughter of one of the other waiters reaches toward me, arms held up, to get closer to my camera. I take her from her mother's arms and dance with her as music surrounds us. I love the relaxed, easy warmth of the spontaneous jam session. The baby plays with us until she can't keep her eyes open. Her mother nurses her to sleep while her dad plays bongos. One of my Dutch companions remarks that on every trip, there are certain quintessential vacation moments. We agree that this is one of them.

Sitting there in the dark, warmed by the music and laughter and Bintang beer, I let my thoughts drift back to another group of happy, lighthearted people: the ones I so envied in Hawaii when I was twenty-five. They, too, were clustered together, listening to music, and drinking beer while watching a tropical sunset. Back then, however, I was observing from the outside, wishing with all my heart that I could be one of those carefree people rather than my overserious, fearful self. And now, here in a fishing village in Bali, I'm living life exactly as I envisioned it all those years ago.

———

After my return from Amed, I hurry back to the guesthouse overlooking the rice paddies of Penestanan. I never tire of hearing Putu Lia's sweet, excited voice announcing, "Mama Leah, Mama Leah!" Our games are mostly physical: playing "Which Hand Is It In?" tossing the inflatable globe, playing with her puppy, sharing songs, and taking videos of Lia's Balinese dancing. Her skills at gesturing and pantomime are amazing, and mine aren't half bad either.

Penestanan has become my home base. If I let Nyoman know when I am returning from an excursion, I will find him and Lia waiting at the foot of the Penestanan steps. Nyoman will hoist my bag onto his shoulder and carry it up the hundred steps to my bungalow. Even when the guest bungalow is not available, he finds me a place to stay in the banjar, and I follow the path to their little house each day for a visit. Putu Lia and Kadek are always at home, and often Nyoman as well.

———

Twenty women from the Threshold Choir have arrived in Ubud. For the past five years, I've been part of an unusual choir. In groups of two to four, our members sing at the bedsides of people who are terminally ill or dying. I treasure the double gift our service offers. For me, singing in harmony is always a joyful uplifting experience. Moreover, seeing the comfort that our carefully curated melodies bring to terminally ill patients and their families is deeply moving. On one of her last days, a frail, white-haired woman told us, "I knew I was about to meet an angel choir, but I didn't expect to hear them before I died."

Our choir's founder, Kate Munger, loves Bali and arranged a two-week trip for a group of interested singers. I knew they would be coming toward the end of my stay in Asia. After months of solo travel, I am especially eager to be part of a group.

We quickly become "Bali sisters." Everywhere we go, we sing. Balinese communities hold a full moon ceremony each month. On the night of the full moon, after an exceedingly hot day, we decide to create our own musical moon ceremony. We gather in our hotel swimming pool, and in three-part harmony, we sing every moon song we know.

A few days later, at a sacred temple, clusters of souvenir sellers persistently follow us, holding out their wares and disrupting the peacefulness by loudly urging us to buy something. Spontaneously, we start singing *tidak mau* (we don't want any) as if it were a lullaby. The hawkers first stare at us, then smile and finally leave us alone.

The choir's trip culminates with a service project for a group of disabled Balinese adults with whom we have been exchanging songs in their language and ours. Some in the group are being trained as artisans. They carve and paint tropical fish to create colorful mobiles. Due to their disabilities most have never seen living fish swimming in water, so we've been enlisted to take them into the sea to snorkel for the first time. We use a beach hammock to lower them one by one from the deck of a boat into the water where a Threshold partner awaits each of them. The physical effort of lowering hammocks filled with heavy bodies is totally worth it when we start hearing shrieks of delight as they spot the wriggling tropical fish they've been carving for years. Later, I ask our Balinese guide, "Why in the world did you choose a bunch of postmenopausal women for this crazy project?"

"Well, I'll tell you why." As I rub my sore back, she explains. "I've been wanting to do this for years, and I've asked dozens of groups. No one but Kate has ever said yes."

My singing sisters have departed, and I am returning to Amed for my final week in Bali. When the transport pulls up in front of Three Brothers Bungalows, one of the children announces, "Mama Leah's back." Soon Kadek comes out to welcome me. With obvious satisfaction, she reports, "Remember that baby girl you helped last month? She is now eating and gaining weight. She is walking and talking. She smiles all day long." With amusement, Kadek says, "I guess she likes your Western medicine better than Bali medicine."

I am delighted for the child. I am also heartened to see how readily global travelers can participate and contribute. Everywhere I have gone, I've met global travelers who are making modest but meaningful contributions. They are volunteering in orphanages, joining community projects, farming, providing disaster relief, and teaching English. (Tutoring English—a simple task for us—can have a huge impact on the lives and prosperity of people in many parts of the world.)

Mother Teresa famously said, "Not all of us can do great things. But we can do small things with great love."

It is one thing to hear the words; it's quite another to live the experience over and over and over. Doing small things in Costa Rica, Guatemala, and Indonesia has not only brought satisfaction; it has made a Nobel Prize feel quite unnecessary.

My time in Bali introduced me to the gift of solitude. There were evenings when I was alone in a guesthouse; days spent walking, often for long distances; periods of time between encounters spent reading or watching the waves; and evenings eating alone in a restaurant, simply tasting my food and noticing what was going on around me.

In Amed, I enjoyed being by myself. I was happy to have the mountains and the warm sea with its brilliant underwater life for company. In the water, I had the *felt experience* of being peaceful and content while alone.

When the choir was in Bali, I learned a new song composed by one of our talented members. Now, as I walk the streets of Ubud, I sing to myself:

My grateful heart, so filled with years of living,
Memories flow by me like petals on a stream,
My grateful heart forgives so many sorrows,
Brings peace that lasts forever, illuminates the dream.

How perfectly the music and lyrics convey my gratitude for these spacious months in Bali. My own sorrows—stemming from an unforgiving story about forfeited opportunities—are gradually being assuaged by a new story of exploration and friendship and this unanticipated blossoming in later life.

Musicians claim that the beauty of music is not just in the notes but in the spaces between them. For me, this has been an unexpected gift of traveling solo: daring to put more space between the notes of my life.

CHAPTER 14

Sex and the Single Spouse

CALIFORNIA

The journey home from Asia feels interminable. From Bali to Singapore to Hong Kong to San Francisco: two days of air travel collapsed into one calendar day as we hurtle through multiple time zones to the other side of the globe. The flight crew captures my confusion perfectly with an announcement wishing us a pleasant evening in San Francisco while clearing our breakfast trays.

Even though I've been excited to see Charley, I grow anxious as our plane approaches San Francisco. *How will it be to see Charley's face at the airport? How will I respond to his body and his desire for mine?*

When I clear customs and emerge, I see Charley holding a bouquet of flowers. My face contorts involuntarily, and suddenly, I'm in tears. They are tears of relief. This uncharacteristic reaction lets me know that I still haven't gotten over the Java earthquake. I have finally made it home to the Bay Area. Back to the San Andreas Fault. Safe at last . . .

I struggle with a feeling of disorientation. Just three days ago, I was walking through the rice paddies in Penestanan, greeting neighbors with "*Selamat pagi.*" Now I am riding up Highway

101 chattering with Charley about my trip and watching familiar urban landmarks whiz by. It takes vigilance to stop putting toilet paper in the wastebasket; I have to keep reminding myself that I'm back in "flush-it-down-the-bowl" land. For several days, I continue to feel naughty whenever I walk into a room with my shoes on. After living on the other side of the world for four months, I experience mental jet lag. When we stop to have a hamburger, there is a TV in the restaurant. "Oh, look," I say to Charley, "they're televising the baseball game from America." Then I remember, "Oh, right—this *is* America."

Directly from the San Francisco airport, we head to a motel in Calistoga. Charley has not only brought flowers but also pillows from our bed at home. I can see he's become more mindful and more capable while living on his own. He proudly acknowledges that in the past year, he has learned to make his own social arrangements, he's developed a liking for opera, and he brings food when invited to a potluck. I am impressed.

On the drive to Calistoga and throughout the next day, I tell Charley about my travel adventures. I share stories about doing relief work, my time in Amed, taking disabled people snorkeling, and helping a failure-to-thrive baby thanks to the CDC doctor we met in Guatemala. After sweet lovemaking, a soak in hot springs, and a bike ride, Charley mentions that he has some adventures of his own to tell me about. I settle onto the bed and ready myself to hear about professional conferences, his reflections on work, or perhaps news about colleagues.

"I have a friend," he says simply.

I am blank for a moment, and then I grasp his meaning. "Someone you are thinking about having sex with?" I ask.

"Yes."

"No kidding—really? Have you had sex with her already?"

"We are definitely ready to."

"Well, I sure called that one wrong," I blurt. "I didn't think you'd take me up on my offer. I knew you liked the idea, but frankly, I thought you'd be way too busy with work to do anything about it." I am silent for a while. I am amazed, surprised, and immensely curious. Then, I speak up. "I have tons of questions. Are you ready for me to ask them"

"Yes."

I want to know where they met. "How did you broach it? Have you kissed? Dated? What is her situation? Does she understand that you are not truly available? How does she feel about that?" Charley answers my questions simply and directly. She's a colleague and lives out of town. She understands the arrangement.

I have two powerful reactions, both of which surprise me. One comes immediately, the other surfaces a few days later. My immediate reaction is to find myself intensely aroused. That my curiosity is piqued does not surprise me; I think that behind my anxieties, I am a genuinely curious person. But I'm astounded at what a huge turn-on this revelation is. Suddenly, I can really feel my love for Charley. I am desirous and possessive. Later, Charley will tell me that he totally anticipated this. Knowing my indecisiveness and my tendency to be uncertain and ambivalent about all my choices, he figured a recommendation from another woman might be reassuring to me. We will laugh about how well Charley knows me. It's something I appreciate about him and treasure about long-term marriage.

———

As the days go by, I keep having more questions. "Would you sleep all night in her bed?"

"No."

"Good!"

But then I'm hit by my second reaction. Charley has often told me that guys, and this includes himself, can think about sex fifty times a day. (Men really *are* a different species.) I ask him,

"When you are thinking about sex those fifty times a day, do you fantasize putting your cock inside her?"

"Yes."

And to my surprise, it is *this* that makes me sad . . . incredibly sad. Bereft even.

How strange that the idea of Charley having sex with another woman when I'm away hasn't threatened me. After all, I'm not around for him to be having sex with. But the possibility that he is fantasizing about having sex with her when I *am* around makes me feel like something that belongs to me is being taken away.

"I still fantasize about having sex with *you* lots and lots," Charley tries to reassure me. "And you know my sexual fantasies were never just about you."

The next morning, waking up in his arms, I tell Charley that I hope he would never spend the whole night with her. I know it's his call, but I wish he would not sleep with her in his arms.

The intensity of my sexual arousal continues to astonish me. Returning to our heavily packed car with groceries, I ask Charley where we can possibly put all these bags. "How about on your lap," he jokes.

"How about on the seat," I retort, "and I'll just give you a lap dance while you drive."

Charley asks what I know about lap dancing, and although I don't know a thing, I seductively promise to show him after dinner what I imagine I know about it.

While Charley is cleaning up from our meal, I start playing a CD of gamelan music and turn down the lights. Then I retreat to the bathroom. I take off my clothes and rummage through my luggage from Asia. I find the wide ceremonial sash from Bali and wrap it around myself—a very mini miniskirt without benefit of underwear. Next comes a tight-fitting black see-through lace blouse that Kadek gifted to me for Balinese ceremonies. (The delicate garment strains across my breasts, but at least I can button it.) From the bathroom, I tell Charley that I am ready for him.

When he comes into the living room, I take on the firm tone of a dominatrix and call out that he is to sit in an armless chair. Then I come dancing into the room and watch his eyes widen. I remember some belly-dance moves from a long-ago dance class. I gyrate to the music, coming closer and closer to the chair. I tell him, "No hands," and proceed to lift my leg and provocatively swing it high over his chair. Facing him and straddling first one of his legs and then the other, I squeeze each of his thighs between my own. Now, I turn my back to him, bend forward, and circle my hips, making my scantily clad buttocks as round as I can. Reflections in the dark window glass guide my movements. Charley is breathing heavily. He is holding the seat of the chair tightly with both hands. He must be wondering about this hot babe who looks a lot like his wife but acts so much sexier. He alternately stares at me and grins with pleasure. I revel in my power over him.

"You may use one hand," I instruct, and as Charley reaches between my legs, I amend my directions: "Above my waist only!" From "one hand" to "two," from "above my waist only" to "anything you desire," I tease and twist and press myself into him, drawing out the excitement until we can hardly stand it.

There is no chance I can pretend this erotic intensity is unrelated to Charley's interest in another woman. I am surprised and amazed, but also curious and reflective. What is it about Charley's sexual desire for someone else that so ignites my erotic imagination?

———

After two days, we move to our group cabin in the Sierras for our summer week. We ride bikes and swim in the little lake nearby. We enjoy slow awakenings, deep kisses, and music Charley has chosen. Vacation Charley is my ideal husband, so different from work Charley. I am supercharged with desire, longing, and passion. Our clothes keep ending up on the floor as we share our open hearts and bodies.

"You are the love of my life," says Charley, gazing into my eyes. "I've waited thirty years to hear this."

We are like a pair of twenty-two-year-olds, surging with hormones, making love over and over. This orgy of mutual desire culminates in the return of my sciatica . . . a rude reminder of my actual age.

After a few days of sumptuous gazing, lovemaking, and sharing sweet nothings, I want time to myself. Delicious as this erotic intimacy has been, I long for a stretch of solo time. Charley appreciates my being clear and direct about needing separateness. He goes for a long bike ride; I idle around the cabin happy just to be on my own.

When Charley returns, I tell him I want to communicate with his woman friend.

"Why? What do you want to tell her?" After I explain, Charley gives me her email address.

Later, when I am alone, I write a note introducing myself and acknowledging her with respect. I spell out my concern. "Neither Charley nor I have ever considered anything like this before. But I want you to know, it's immensely important to me that it not harm our marriage."

Her reply is prompt . . . and lands like a slap in the face. She is clear about the ground rules but wants no contact with me except to let her know if something dire happens to my husband.

Suddenly, alarm bells are going off. Something feels very wrong here, and I grow increasingly upset. I have trouble focusing on anything else. Charley's friend is absorbing way too much of my attention and emotions.

I start to feel angry. At first, I'm angry with Charley's lady friend for her cold, insensitive response to my email. Then I realize I am angry with Charley. When we originally negotiated this sabbatical almost two years ago, we talked about extramarital sex in terms of a meaningless hookup. Connecting with a professional colleague, even an out-of-state colleague, is *not* a meaningless hookup. No way!

I've been so caught up, first in surprise and disbelief, then in erotic titillation and most recently in preoccupation, that I got distracted from the ground rules to our agreement. As they come back, I feel increasingly upset.

Now I have many more questions for Charley. "Are you having ongoing contact with her?"

"Yes, by email."

"How often do you email each other?"

"Daily."

"Charley, what you're describing doesn't exactly fit my idea of a meaningless hookup."

"Look, I told you I would not get involved; I haven't, and I won't."

Soon I am beset by another intense reaction. I have a huge desire to read Charley's email. The urge to snoop is overwhelming. We've returned home from the Sierras, and Charley is back at work. I want to know more about his exchanges with this woman. I will *not* collaborate in being shut out of my own husband's sex life. Yet I have never been sneaky or snoopy, and I don't like seeing myself become so. I try to get into his email account; Charley has changed his password.

I sit on my meditation cushion and ask for guidance—and for protection from that demon, depression. In truth, I feel deeply confused. How did something we negotiated so carefully turn into such a whirlwind of intense emotions? How did I misjudge Charley so thoroughly? And what in the world happened between my freewheeling single days and the present to make me react so differently? Each time I start to think about these questions, I return to the fact that I never signed on for Charley to engage in a daily email relationship with another woman. This is *not* what we agreed to!

It is easy to be angry with Charley for not knowing the difference between a one-night stand and an ongoing involvement with a professional colleague. As I sit with my righteous indignation, up floats an image of the black-and-white checkered fabric that is ubiquitous in Bali. I remember my conversations with Jassi as we sat on her patio drinking ginger tea. Life is not black or white. Within each of us, there is goodness and shadow. Charley and I were both seeking ways to make our long separation work out.

The following day, I tell Charley that I may not be able to handle his having sex with another woman after all. He responds with frustration and anger. He repeats that he isn't getting involved and that I needn't feel concerned. "Hey, Charley," I say. "Emailing a woman every day sounds a lot like an ongoing relationship to me. Besides, you're not always connected with your feelings. I can often sense what you're feeling before *you* can." The more I talk, the more upset I feel. "Frankly, I don't think you have a clue what 'not getting involved' really means."

At this point, I realize that I am in way over my head. I suggest to Charley that I get a consultation for myself with a therapist we know. He is smart and astute, and we know he's fond of us both. Charley agrees that this is a good idea.

Sitting in the oversize brown leather chair in Eric Greenleaf's office, I barely finish describing the arrangement Charley and I are embarking on when Eric, who is ordinarily a good and patient listener, jumps in. His message is clear. "This is the stupidest plan I've heard about in a long time!" Since I trust him not to be moralistic for its own sake, I listen with interest.

"It is not the first time I've consulted on such matters," Eric begins. "Here's the problem with sex play as I see it. In relating to you, Charley must pretend not to have feelings for this woman. However, in relating to his out-of-town partner, he *has* to convey feelings for her. This puts him in a considerable bind. He's in a situation where he cannot be fully authentic or forthright with either one of you."

Eric is convinced that the only reason I ever agreed to Charley having sex with someone else was to not feel so beholden to him. "Well, that's part of it," I agree. "But also, he was saying yes to a precious dream of mine, and I really wanted to reciprocate. I knew Charley wouldn't want to go without sex for months at a time, and I figured that if he didn't get emotionally involved, this was something I could give him."

Now Eric takes on the tone of a teacher. "You've instructed Charley to have no feelings for this sexual partner. What you're asking of him is impossible. You misperceive him; Charley believes in relationship," Eric points out. "The man you love is a related guy. He is all *about* feelings. And you wouldn't want it any other way."

Eric is right. I wouldn't want it any other way. Furthermore, I relish this view of my husband. Charley gets so caught up in his work and is so self-contained that sometimes I think close relationships aren't that important to him. Eric's perspective is comforting. "Charley has come as close as he possibly can in trying to do the impossible. You need to apologize and tell him, 'I'm sorry for asking the impossible of you.'"

At this point, I describe my email exchange with Charley's long-distance colleague. "I want to be able to keep out of this relationship, but I can't."

"Of course you can't. The pair bond is a human way of relating," Eric observes. "Don't mess with it. You need to find some other way to manage your indebtedness to him."

"You mean . . . like gratitude?"

"Now *there's* an idea!"

Driving home from Eric's office, I again think about black and white and the devotion to balance that is woven into Balinese culture. In our culture, we speak about our *shadow*: those parts of ourselves that we fail to fully recognize. For me, it was the fact that I was playing with sexual fire and pretending it was no big deal. For Charley, it was misinterpreting the ground rules about not getting involved. We each had a role in believing that this was a viable arrangement.

Charley is eager to hear what Eric had to say. I relay his feedback and then deliver my apology as earnestly as I can. "I guess *I* was out of touch with my feelings when I assumed I could be fine while you had a sexual encounter with somebody else. I was so excited when it looked like I might really get to travel the world, and I was so eager to offer you anything that would help you want to say yes that I didn't realize that—for me—the sexual revolution is over. It was reckless on my part. Charley, I am so sorry." I ask him if he will please extend his apologies to his colleague and give up the idea of having sex outside our marriage.

Charley agrees without protest. Given his inevitable frustration and disappointment, I am touched by how graciously he sets aside his plans.

Both Charley and I are introspective people. At its worst, this quality tends toward self-absorption and difficulty taking action. At its best, it fosters the ability to sit with intense feelings and impulses. It supports the kind of reflection and honesty that can turn a potential conflagration into an opportunity for intimacy. I'm grateful that in this way, the two of us are well matched.

I would love to say that our white-hot marital passion has persisted, but of course it wouldn't be true. Instead, it quickly subsides into the normal and quite satisfactory fluctuations of long-term monogamy.

CHAPTER 15

Dreams and Disappointments

COSTA RICA

I'm sitting on my bed at home, a semicircle of tantalizing travel guides surrounding me like a rainbow. Morocco, Cuba, South Africa, Colombia, Peru: each destination is alluring. In a month, I'll begin the final phase of my sabbatical, but I can't decide where I want to go. I eventually opt to start with another two weeks of language school in Costa Rica and conclude my sabbatical four months later in Guatemala. There's no need to determine what I'll do in between. Leaving things open is part of the adventure.

I've begun to feel restless. I'm frequently irritated with Charley. *Is this the same guy I couldn't keep my hands off of just a few months ago?* Over dinner one night, I tell Charley that it's time for me to go.

"We've gotten thoroughly sick of each other," I inform him.

His response catches me by surprise. "No," he counters. "I think we've gotten lonely for each other."

"Where do you get that idea?" I ask with a challenging edge to my voice.

"You haven't been the same since your last trip to Arizona. I think you're worried about leaving your mother."

I feel momentarily confused, and then I understand. "Oh, honey! That totally makes sense. You know, being married to a psychoanalyst occasionally has its perks."

On my most recent trip to visit my mother, I could see she was fed up with pain from arthritis and vertigo and dementia. I remember a particularly telling conversation. We were in her study. Mother lowered herself into a chair with her habitual "unhh." Once settled, she struggled to find the right word:

"Please remind me, what do you call those doctors who take care of animals?"

"Do you mean *veterinarian*?"

"Yes, that's it." Then, in a quiet voice, she confided: "Sometimes I wish I had a veterinarian instead of an internist." Even with dementia, she couldn't be clearer that she's ready to be put down.

I talk with my brother and suggest postponing my trip. He encourages me to go and assures me he'll let me know if anything changes. I thank him. "But please remember, if anything changes, I *want* to come home. Latin America will always be there." Although our mom no longer needs hospice care, we both know that little by little, we are losing her.

As my departure date approaches, a familiar pattern emerges. I grow obsessively busy with paper clutter, household matters, and eldercare arrangements. Although these are useful tasks, I'm acting like I need to leave my affairs in order.

What if I get malaria, or worse, dengue fever? What if I go to Colombia and then get kidnapped? Clinical training and my own family history have sensitized me to issues of attachment and separation. My concerns sure look like separation anxiety—the fear that harm will come to me if I go away. But in fact, I am also dealing with separation *guilt*. Camouflaged underneath worry about my own safety lurks the fear that I will cause harm to someone I love if I leave them. I know Charley will be fine if I go away for a while. But I'm not so sure about my mom.

Watching myself rush around, I think about the daily

offerings the Balinese make to appease the gods. I envision grace-ful Kadek preparing her offerings of flowers and incense and a portion of the day's food. I see her moving a stick of incense like a wand, drawing circles of fragrant smoke. It occurs to me that I, too, am making offerings to the gods. I offer my frenzy to appease the god of hearth and home, the god of marriage, and especially the god of frail parents.

Despite my fears, I know I must keep moving forward. Life has offered me this second chance to make a dream come true. I mustn't let the icy stabs of terror I experience before each depar-ture hold me back. I know my mom is in good hands. I also know that in a few short weeks, I will get on a plane and—safely out of sight of those I love most—I will start having the time of my life.

I arrive in Samara in time for a late-afternoon swim. December in Northern California feels far away as I push through the gentle breakers until I reach deeper water, where I can stretch out achy limbs stiffened by hours of airplane sitting. Making gentle dol-phin undulations, I start to play. And soon, the pelicans arrive. They sit on the water in an almost perfect circle, evenly spaced except for one opening. Very, very slowly, I swim toward them. Giving the pelicans time to get used to my presence, I attempt to join the circle. They allow me to get quite close; however, at the point where I might enter their fishing territory, they shift their formation. But at least they don't fly away.

In the water, I feel like my truest self. And no wonder: we all began life swimming in a warm amniotic sea. Floating on my back, I give a deep exhalation. Finally, I can relax.

There are no other students at my language level this week, so Melvin becomes my private instructor. I'm disappointed. I miss the hilarity Melvin brings to a classroom of students, and I miss having structured lessons and homework. On the other hand, we are free to converse—in Spanish, of course—about whatever we want. Most days we go for coffee and then walk along the beach or sit in the air-conditioned classroom and talk. Melvin has never been to the United States, but he's heard a lot about it and wants to know more. With considerable grammatical and vocabulary help, we discuss relationships, hallucinogens, and attitudes toward sexuality in our respective countries.

As we walk along the beach one morning, Melvin tells me to describe my daily life at home. I mention that when I wake up in the morning, Charley has left for work, and that he often comes home quite late at night. Turning to me, Melvin asks, "*¿Es aburido?*" I struggle to remember the word. Then it comes. Melvin has asked, "Is it boring?" Or perhaps "Is *he* boring?"

I am speechless, shocked. After a long silence, I answer quietly, embarrassed, "Sí."

No one has ever asked if I'm bored in my marriage, and I have never acknowledged it . . . even to myself. Suddenly, I feel dizzy. I am hot with shame and confusion. I change the subject, and we return to the classroom.

After class, I head to the beach. All afternoon, I wrestle with Melvin's audacious question. I feel flattened, as if I'd been slammed by a wave. My hero husband has suddenly become an intolerable partner.

I've had this response before. I can be going along fine, and then a critical remark about Charley or a flash of envy over someone else's relationship will trigger my disappointments and throw me into a frenzy of dissatisfaction.

My thoughts start racing. *Why would I choose someone who isn't comfortable unless he's working? Someone who acts as if relaxation or play aren't important? Someone who says he loves me but keeps his distance. If Charley is boring, maybe it's because he keeps so much of himself to himself!*

Fortunately for both of us, Charley is not here. Sitting alone on a thick log near the water, I feel simultaneously inflamed with agitation and weighed down. Despite my distress, I hear the sound of the waves moving toward the shore and then retreating. I watch the children playing—the little ones in the sand and the older ones in the surf. Finally I become aware of the absurd contrast between my mood and the sparkling beauty around me—and torment gives way to thoughtful reflection.

My disappointments are real. And they hurt! But these disappointments are chronic. They alone can't explain what periodically pulls me into the undertow. I think what sucks me under is *shame*. Shame that for all my decades of effort and persistence I haven't been able to turn this relationship into one we both enjoy and I can feel proud of. Melvin's question leaves me feeling exposed.

Charley must surely harbor his own share of disappointments with me. I know I'm not an easy partner . . . probably sometimes impossible. However, our ways of dealing with disappointment are different. Charley keeps his disappointments to himself— maybe even *from* himself; I insist on shouting mine through a bullhorn. Neither approach is effective.

As the gentle waves move in and out, I see how the two of us are bound together in a mutually depriving dance. I want us to be together and dance with abandon. But Charley's dance moves are stiff and awkward. I start to wish I had a different dance partner. I get tight-lipped and critical, oblivious to my impact on the dance. Charley steps back for protection and loses the rhythm. I make no secret of my scorn. Charley, understandably, steps back further. We move around the dance floor constrained by our habitual set of clumsy moves, neither of us getting what we need to thrive.

I think about our predicament. Our collection of disappointments will probably stay with us. But Charley is by no means boring—far from it. He is smart and intellectually curious and well-informed. I am not a fool to have married him. I am a spouse in a complicated marriage.

I sit on the beach for a long time feeling the sun on my skin, the prickle of sand on the back of my legs. I watch birds float on the updraft. Lulled by the rhythmic sounds of the surf, I start to imagine the possibility of a new dance.

———

I'm eager to renew my friendship with Hazel and her family. After my first week in Samara, Hazel invites me to spend the weekend in the tiny *pueblito* of Santa Marta. Santa Marta is about forty minutes from the coast up a steep, unpaved road. This is where she and Guillermo both grew up and where they are currently building a house. Just mention Santa Marta and all four of them have joy in their voices and radiant smiles on their faces. The children are like jumping beans as their *papi* packs the jeep. I have no idea what to expect, but I feel privileged to be invited.

We drive up and up a bumpy, dusty road into the hills. As the temperature grows cooler, Hazel says, "I'm afraid you may see Santa Marta and think, 'Ugh, *que feo!*'" (How ugly!) I realize my friend is brave to invite me into her village and home, having no notion of my North American standards or judgments.

Eventually, we pass the sign announcing Santa Marta. One of the first houses is a small wooden structure with chickens strutting in the yard. Guillermo stops and honks his horn. A woman appears, and he calls out what sounds to me like "Blah, blah, blah, *pollo*, blah, blah." I still can't follow speedy conversations, but I wonder if Guillermo is shopping for dinner from the window of his jeep. Sure enough, the woman goes into her house and returns with a bagged chicken that she hands through the window. Guillermo sets it on the floor of the jeep, and we continue.

A little further on, my attention is drawn to a picturesque A-frame house on our left. It looks like a Swiss chalet with planters of cheerful red flowers. The front door stands open. Guillermo drives up to this house, and Hazel announces with quiet pride, "*Aquí está nuestra casa.*" (Here is our house.)

Juan Luis and Paola bound through the open front door, racing straight through the house and out the back door. Behind Hazel and Guillermo's new house is the home of Tita, Hazel's mother. Her father, who died last year, is buried in the cemetery across the street within view of Hazel's front door.

Soon, half a dozen people have drifted through the open door to greet Juan Luis and scoop up Paola, covering her with hugs and kisses and exclamations about her beauty. "Yes," Guillermo responds to my question, they *do* know everyone in Santa Marta.

The family's nearly finished house is . . . well, it's perfect. It is compact and cozy. A single open area serves as living room, dining room, and kitchen. The floor is made of creamy ceramic tile; the walls are painted a sunny golden yellow. Dark teakwood frames the windows. There are three small bedrooms downstairs. A ladder leads upstairs to another large open space plus one more bedroom. The house is modest in size, yet everything is well designed and functional. No wonder Hazel feels proud of their home.

Years ago, Hazel explains, Guillermo had a dream in which he envisioned this house. It became his ambition to build a house precisely like his dream in every detail. I smile with fondness for my young friend. "And now your family is living in his dream."

"Yes, we are happily living in his dream," Hazel agrees.

Hazel insists that I sleep in their bedroom. In addition to the bed, there is a single shelf fastened to the wall. On it are a copy of the Bible and a framed picture of Mother Teresa. Next to them, Hazel has placed a snapshot she took last year; in the photo, I am hugging and reading to the children. I am touched by her thoughtful welcome.

I realize I've met this family at a moment in time when Guillermo, Hazel, and I are each bringing important dreams to life, dreams we've been gestating for many years. Seeing the physical completion of Guillermo's dream helps give shape to my own.

CHAPTER 16

Heart's Desire

COLOMBIA

"Let me know where you'd like me to meet you," Charley proposed before my departure. He has cleared two weeks in his schedule, leaving me to choose the destination for our travels. I am pleased by his confidence that I will plan a good adventure.

I call Charley one hot, humid evening from Samara's single pay phone. Over the static, I tell him, "Charley, I'd like to go with you to Colombia."

Charley is surprised. "Why Colombia?"

"Well, there are two reasons. I've been meeting European travelers who rave about Colombia. Many say it is their favorite country in Latin America."

"That's kind of surprising," Charley responds. "So, what is your other reason?"

"Well," I confess, "I'm nervous about traveling alone in Colombia. There are still occasional abductions. And if I get abducted, I know you'll feel obliged to pay my ransom. But if we're together, we're less likely to be kidnapped. And if we are, I know exactly what to say."

"What's that?"

"*¡Si pueden obtener dinero de nuestros hijos, lo más poder a ustedes!*" I *think* that means "If you can get money from our kids, the more power to you!"

Joking aside, I feel considerably safer exploring Colombia with Charley. I like the idea of our having a new adventure together, being a little braver as a couple than either of us would be on our own.

———

The sound of vibrant drumming lures us into a plaza on our first evening in the historic colonial city of Cartagena. A troupe of Afro-Caribbean dancers are performing. We join the crowd of people clustered around the performers. I need to stand on tiptoe to see the shirtless men and the women in colorful muu-muu-like dresses. The barefoot young dancers are moving their bodies at a furious pace. Shoulder-shimmies, pelvic thrusts, and circling hips, all at a tempo faster than my eyes can track. I have never seen anything like this. My excitement must be apparent because a man standing near us leans over to explain the dance is called *cumbia*. Between dances, the women change costumes right there in front of everyone, removing their long dresses to reveal short, frilly skirts over black dance shorts. I can scarcely fathom the amount of energy these dancers expend during their forty-five-minute performance. Later in the evening, we will find them in another plaza repeating their incredible exertion.

The following morning, we explore the old city with leisurely curiosity. The graceful colonial architecture throughout this part of Cartagena is a reminder of Colombia's historical ties with Spain. I am charmed to see Colombianos of every skin color gathered in the plazas; but my pleasure is tempered when I realize the slave trade played a large role in this beautiful array of flesh tones.

At lunchtime, Charley and I choose a café popular with the

locals. All the tables are packed, so the hostess seats us at a table with a late-middle-aged gentleman. Eduardo is very outgoing and speaks perfect English. He is educated, politically aware, and reflective. Over lunch, Charley steers the conversation toward politics. Eduardo jumps right in. He explains that the drug trade provides funding for the paramilitary forces, helping to perpetuate Colombia's ongoing political violence. Charley asks Eduardo to tell us about the drug trade. And now the conversation comes to life.

Eduardo explains that although Colombian by birth, he lived in the United States, mostly in Miami, from age twelve until age forty. Now our table companion mentions casually that he himself used to be in the drug business. Of course, we are fascinated. Eduardo clearly loves having an audience, and he begins telling us stories.

Apparently, he was a major dealer, primarily in marijuana but also cocaine. Eduardo tells us matter-of-factly that he's been arrested at various times and has spent a total of twelve years in prison in the United States. He is philosophical about this too. "It's one of the costs of my profession." When we ask what it is like being in prison, he answers, "People tend to do in prison pretty much what they do on the outside." In response to my quizzical look, he says, "In my case, I read and studied law and tutored other inmates." We learn that he was eventually deported from the United States back to Colombia. He sorely misses the States and the company of Norte Americanos.

Eduardo astounds us with tales of brazen daring. Some of the adventures are his own; others are exploits of fellow drug runners. One of the more dramatic involves hiring a helicopter from a TV station to deliver drugs. Another one entails landing a plane at night without lights on the airstrip of a military base. Believable? Unbelievable? We'll never know.

Charley and I find Eduardo charming. At the same time, I am uncomfortable being charmed by a narcotrafficker. But

Eduardo keeps surprising us. While answering my questions about being a drug runner, Eduardo states his personal work ethic: "I would never, *ever* ask an employee to do anything I wouldn't be willing to do myself."

———

Following lunch, Eduardo insists that we mustn't leave town before he shows us "the real Cartagena." There are dramatic extremes of rich and poor outside the walls of the World Heritage Site, he explains. He will come in a taxi in the morning before our flight to Bogotá.

We are packed to leave when, true to his word, Eduardo shows up in a taxi. As we exit the original walled city of colonial Cartagena, our enthusiastic self-appointed guide directs the taxi driver to the neighborhood where he grew up. Eduardo points out his old house and his school. This area is designated Level five. There is no pretense here: Cartagena's socio-economic stratification is explicit. Proceeding to level six, we drive past magnificent homes. Then we head down to Level One and Level Two. Eduardo clearly wants us to have a good look at this slice of life. The houses are tiny wooden structures barely above sea level; smelly, brackish water practically laps at the already decrepit walls of some. Primitive outhouses in the yards testify to the lack of indoor plumbing.

After the taxi drops us at the airport and we say goodbye, Charley and I look at each other in amazement. In addition to the pure novelty of encountering a Colombian former drug runner, our stereotypes are exploded by getting acquainted with a retired narcotrafficker who is sensitive and insightful with a strong social conscience. Eduardo has certainly advanced our education as global citizens. The encounter will make us slower to think simplistically about complex issues.

———

The region called the Zona Cafetera sits on the slopes of a long string of steep mountains called the Cordillera Central. The weather here is cooler than in humid Cartagena. Our homestay is in a large, rambling house on the outskirts of the city of Armenia. When we arrive late at night, a party is in full swing. Our host has forewarned us there will be music and noise until about midnight. We unpack and lie in bed listening to the loud dance music until we fall asleep. For each of us, it brings back memories of being in our childhood bedrooms listening to our parents having dinner parties downstairs.

The house where we are staying is entirely open to the air. Under the roof and bamboo framing, only the bedrooms, bathrooms, and kitchen are enclosed within walls. Our host, Marina, tells us that she designed this house herself. The few interior walls are painted in bold, vibrant colors and display original art created by talented friends or gathered during Marina's travels. The house overlooks a steep, lush valley, and the vistas are magnificent. This unique house is only the beginning of an out-of-the-ordinary homestay.

We are fascinated by our host and her remarkable family. Marina is a strong, competent woman, tall and thin with muscled arms. She and her siblings are smart and worldly. Members of their family have been landowners in this breathtaking region for generations. We have rarely spent time with people who are this wealthy—or this hip.

Here in the Cafetera, the cool, crisp air and warm sun are ideal for growing coffee. They are also ideal for morning walks though the coffee fincas. We are starting to understand why European travelers rave about Colombia.

One afternoon, while I rest and read, Charley hikes through the valley that we've been viewing from above. He is gone for several hours and returns, radiant and happy, with reports of orchids, quetzal birds, hummingbirds, and parrots.

A few days into our stay, Marina informs us apologetically about an impromptu party happening in the evening. "You are most welcome to join in the festivities." Charley and I eagerly accept.

The party is a large one. The open-air great room is filled with lively Afro-Cuban music and dancing guests. Lured by the music, Charley and I dance together, keeping the beat and smiling with surprise and delight. Later in the evening, Marina brings us into the kitchen, where guests are eating and drinking. A smaller group has congregated in a lovely outdoor sitting area furnished with comfortable-looking sofas covered with nubby white upholstery fabric. The smell of marijuana wafts in from outside, but we are not invited to participate.

Over breakfast the following morning, Marina suggests ideas for excursions that Charley and I might want to take. One option is a mountainous area with magnificent hot springs. It has a series of natural pools right in the ground, warm waterfalls, and a river flowing by the hot pools. Of course, this is what we choose, and Marina arranges for us to travel to Termales San Vicente. Our destination will turn out to be the best and most romantic hot springs we have ever soaked in.

As we wait for our taxi, I can't resist teasing one of the guests from the night before. "All of you were so hospitable with your wine and food and entertainment. But I noticed no one offered us whatever you were smoking outside."

"You only needed to ask," the young man stammers apologetically.

I laugh and shake my head. "I was only teasing."

Marina apologizes. She was dismayed about her guests smoking weed, not knowing if it would make us uncomfortable or, worse, offended.

The young man quickly excuses himself and retreats down the path with its swaying palms and vines of night-blooming jasmine. Seemingly seconds later, he returns and hands me a perfectly rolled joint.

"You'll want this for the hot springs," he explains.

"Or maybe for my stay in a Colombian jail," I retort.

"You can hide it on yourself in case you are stopped," he assures me. "They rarely search women, usually only men. And even if they find it, just slip them a couple of dollars, and they'll be on their way."

I prepare to return my unwelcome gift, but at this precise moment, our taxi pulls up. Not wanting to make a scene, I slip the joint into my bra.

As Charley and I get into the taxi, there is a rattling exchange of Spanish between Marina and the driver. Apparently, we are heading toward a dangerous part of Colombia. Marina carefully writes down the name of our taxi driver and the license plate number before we leave. She will follow up by phone to inform people at the hot springs that we are on our way, and she will call later to make sure we've arrived safely.

There are good reasons for these precautions. At the party, Marina introduced us to a woman whose father had been kidnapped. She pointed out another woman who herself had been abducted. Our host explained that this woman had recently escaped from the guerillas after seven months in captivity. She'd stayed physically fit by exercising in her jail cell so the one time she was left unguarded, she was able to run like hell.

Clearly, this country has been traumatized. Throughout our travels in Colombia, we are repeatedly asked, "*¿Cómo le parece?*" (How do you like it?) Behind the question, I sense a desire for affirmation: *Yes, you really are a lovely people, and you live in a beautiful country, and you do not deserve to be feared or shunned by the United States.* Given that we meet no other American travelers during our time in Colombia, Charley and I find ourselves in the role of affirming witnesses and ambassadors.

Riding toward the hot springs, I feel burdened by the marijuana cigarette pressing against the underside of my left breast. I have little desire to smoke marijuana, but especially not in Colombia. "I wonder if I should just slip some money into the other cup for a bribe," I whisper to Charley in jest.

Not ten minutes later, we hear a siren and are pulled over at a police roadblock. A machine-gun-armed military policeman peers into the driver's window. Here I am, with illegal drugs in my bra. Now I know what "cold sweat" means. I remain outwardly calm. The policeman keeps talking with the driver and never looks at us. Apparently, the policeman stopped us to chastise our driver for crossing a double yellow line while passing a truck on the curvy road. There follows a lengthy, mutually polite debate about whether it really *was* a double yellow line. Eventually, the military policeman settles for a warning; the driver responds with several "*muy amables*" (you're very kind), and we are on our way again. It feels good to breathe!

The ride through the mountainous terrain is psychedelic without any need for hallucinogens. The grassy slopes are so vividly green they appear to be vibrating. In the distance, grazing black-and-white cattle offer a startling contrast to the astonishing green. The sky is perfectly clear; the air is fresh. As we approach the hot springs, we see soldiers with submachine guns protecting the entrance. Even this sobering touch cannot diminish our excitement. Charley and I adore hot springs.

Some of the most romantic and relaxing moments in our marriage have been spent soaking in hot springs. However, for sheer natural beauty, abundance of soaking options, and moments of lyrical intimacy, Termales San Vicente, high in the mountains of Colombia, surpasses them all.

After we stash our clothes—and the dreaded marijuana cigarette—in a locker, Charley and I spend the rest of the day moving from pool to pool. We start by swimming leisurely laps in the warm water of a large cement swimming pool. After that, we follow a path downhill where a pipe, protruding from the pool above, delivers a cascade of warm water from a height of fifteen feet. There is a single white plastic chair under the flow of water. Charley and I take turns sitting under the warm, pounding waterfall. The feel of that warm water forcefully massaging my head is a sensation my body has memorized and will not forget.

Next, paralleling a cool stream, we find a series of deep and spacious hot pools right in the ground, each circular pool made attractive and comfortable by the addition of sand on the bottom and a perimeter of natural rock. We soak and talk quietly with groups of friendly Colombians and English-speaking Europeans.

It's easy to forget about the guards with machine guns as we move slowly from one natural pool to the next. At the end of a beautiful afternoon spent soaking in every pool but one, we follow our little printed map across a wooden bridge and into the woods in search of Heart's Desire—San Vicente's most remote and unstructured pool. As we hike, I feel incredibly close to Charley. I am proud and happy that we are exploring Colombia together, especially at a time when it's still a little risky to do so.

Following a trail, we find the pool nestled among the trees. It turns out that Heart's Desire is small and extremely shallow. I lower myself into the tepid and slightly muddy water; it barely covers my shoulders. My first reaction is disappointment: "Heart's desire?" But by now I am utterly relaxed, and my own heart is wide open. I see the humor in the situation. I think about my painful response to Melvin's suggestion that living with Charley sounded boring. I contrast that experience with this joyful day soaking in Colombian hot springs with my husband.

Yes, it is perfectly perfect that this lukewarm, murky pool should be called "Heart's Desire." It reminds me I'm not the only spouse who is well matched in some respects while sadly mismatched in others. I am not alone in having essential needs that are met within my marriage and other equally essential ones that go unmet. Yes, I am married to a man who wouldn't accompany me on my enticing, scary sabbatical. Given how many of *his* ventures I've supported, I have good reason to be resentful. However, I am also married to a man who will tolerate long absences while I pursue a compelling dream on my own. I'm married to a man who is proud of me and eager to visit, and who is partnering me right now in growing gutsier.

Come to think of it, I *love* that this muddy pool is called "Heart's Desire."

CHAPTER 17

Repairing the Past

CUBA

"Cuba?" asks my daughter when I call her from Colombia. "Why do you want to go to Cuba?"

"Well, I guess partly because I'm not supposed to."

"I thought so."

But in truth, my reasons for wanting to visit Cuba run much deeper. I know Cuba is on the cusp of change, and I want to experience Fidel Castro's Cuba before those changes take place. Castro is approaching the end of his life. Our long US embargo makes no sense in a post-communist world and will surely be lifted soon. There's another reason. I've heard that Cubans are very happy people. I understand there is music everywhere, music and dance. I am eager to hear the music, learn the dances, and join in the happiness. Finally and most importantly, I want to better understand Cuba's history during the 1960s. I don't know why this matters so much to me, but it does.

—

On the day of Charley's departure, we wake up and hold each other tight. I won't be seeing him again for more than two months. He is returning to San Francisco, and I have a ticket to Cuba by way of Venezuela on the cheapest airline I can find. Hugging Charley, I briefly feel devastated. Through the tightness in my chest, I remind myself that I've planned all along to progress from easier to harder challenges. And right now, going to Cuba feels *hard*. It not only means leaving Charley, but it also means defying my country's prohibition against travel to Cuba. Even though I'm scared, I marvel that I've gone from being that compliant, inhibited young girl . . . to this.

——————

During my layover in Venezuela, I have the kind of travel experience that inspires people to never leave home again! When we land in Caracas, I follow the other travelers to the luggage carousel. Passengers around me pick up their bags and depart. Mine isn't there. The area empties; the carousel stops. I go to the airline counter for help, but it is unattended. My bag is missing, and I am alone.

The Caracas airport is modern and clean and air conditioned beyond endurance. Passengers shiver with their hands pressed between their knees; couples huddle together for warmth. I know better than to leave the airport without my suitcase in a country known for rampant theft. A fellow passenger, a young English-speaking Cubana, says that budget travelers sometimes stay in the airport overnight because the fees to leave and reenter are exorbitant. She plans to stay, and I'm welcome to join her. But I'm only wearing a thin sundress with spaghetti straps. I am freezing. My sweater is packed in my missing luggage. Staying overnight in the airport is out of the question.

What happens next is like a sitcom grafted onto *Night of the Living Dead*. My bag is not downstairs. It is also not upstairs.

A guard, speaking in insanely fast Spanish, tells me to go back downstairs. No bag. "Your bag is definitely upstairs," another airport employee says. Upstairs: still no suitcase. Now, a different employee tells me in Spanish I barely comprehend, "You cannot get your suitcase unless you clear customs. But if you go downstairs, you won't be permitted to come back up." All this information is delivered without a glimmer of concern or any inclination to help.

The nighttime airport grows increasingly deserted. By now I am hungry, and the straps of my pack are digging painfully into my shoulders. After an hour's runaround, an actual employee of the airline, Aeropostal, shows up. He agrees to get my suitcase and writes down all my information. An hour later, he has not come back. By now, two hours have passed in the freezing airport. It is 11:00 p.m.

I remember seeing an unattended information desk downstairs. I no longer care about the guard's warning. I trudge slowly down the steps. Amazingly, an attractive, well-dressed woman is there. She is bright and efficient and speaks the first slow, clear Spanish I've heard all evening. She says the situation is preposterous. She pulls out a walkie-talkie and leaves after promising me she'll work on it.

By now, my feet hurt, and I have a spectacular headache from walking around the airport with the backpack pulling on my neck and shoulders. I am tired, hungry, and acutely aware that I really don't speak Spanish. I miss Charley. I want to get out of Venezuela and never return. No one has been downright rude, but except for this woman, they have all been colossally indifferent.

Suddenly, a man starts shouting at me. This must be who the sympathetic woman found to help me. He unlocks the door to a basement level and grumpily leads me down. By the time I have followed him down four dark flights of stairs, I'm feeling distinctly uncomfortable. I am alone with a strange man in the bowels of the Caracas airport. For the first time on my sabbatical, I sense I may be in danger. I tell the man, "*Esto me parece muy estraño.*" (This feels very strange.) I am keeping a half flight of stairs between us. At this point he blows up, rapidly firing at me what probably translates as "I've been in this business for thirty years and I'm busting my butt for you, lady, and all you can say is '*muy estraño*'!" When we reach the basement, he calls out. Someone appears and reports that my luggage isn't there. We trudge back up the four flights of stairs.

When we emerge, a uniformed airport employee is holding my suitcase. Beside him is a taxi driver who has been waiting outside with my bag all this time. Apparently, he took the initiative to retrieve it from the carousel in hopes of a hefty fare for driving its owner to the capital. When, instead of requesting the hourlong drive into Caracas, I direct him to a nearby budget hotel, he looks deflated. But I'm too tired for empathy. Once inside my room, I fall into bed fully clothed.

Five short hours later, I am back at the airport, standing in a long line. Forty-five minutes after that, I reach the check-in counter. The attendant reaches out her hand. "Your visa?"

This is the first I've heard about needing a visa for a layover in Venezuela. "I have no visa."

She jerks her head toward another long line. "Buy one there."

Finally, after I make it back to the counter, she asks to see my continuing ticket after Cuba.

"I will be purchasing it in Cuba," I explain.

"No," she says. "You can't go through immigration to leave Venezuela without a ticket out of Havana. You will have to go to a travel agency."

Exhausted, on the verge of tears, I say in my clearest, slowest Spanish, "I am only in transit through this country. I have had no dinner; I have had no breakfast. Please, Señora, will you help me?" The woman dismisses me with a shrug.

Finally, I am saved . . . by the black market. A young fellow approaches me and offers his help. Do I want to return to Venezuela? "Never!" I reply emphatically. "After Cuba, I'm going to Mexico."

"Come with me," he instructs and leads me behind the check-in counter to a small office filled with Mexicana Airline employees. There I explain my situation, and in five minutes, a cheerful woman has set me up with a reservation to Mexico City a month from now. Back at the check-in counter of Aeropostal, I pay the exorbitant departure tax almost gratefully. Our plane leaves an hour late. Adiós, Venezuela!

As our plane heads toward Cuba, I think about the prospect of being apprehended by US immigration officials when I return home. The fine for illegally entering Cuba is daunting. My experience in Venezuela has only increased my nervousness. All the way from Caracas to Havana, I practice the phrase I will need to avoid being caught and penalized when I return to my own country: "*Por favor, no selles mi pasaporte; Por favor, no séllalo . . .*" (Please don't stamp my passport.)

"*Por supuesto,*" responds the Cuban immigration officer with his direct gaze and clear green eyes. (Of course.) He stamps a small disposable piece of paper and hands it to me.

"*Su pasaporte, mi amor,*" sings out a plump, full-breasted woman at the entrance to customs. (Your passport, my love.) She smiles warmly and waves me through customs. I am flooded with relief and surprise. So, *this* is Cuba.

———

I was a bashful college freshman in 1962. There was a gorgeous boy in our class named Jorge Bacardi. He had large dark eyes, glossy black hair, and classic Latin good looks. I heard that he was from Cuba and that his family made liquor or something. As he walked across campus, the prettiest, most confident girls often accompanied him. I would watch wistfully. I think he said hi to me a couple of times. But I was the serious, unsmiling girl who rode her bike to the library every day and stayed till closing time, slogging through endless reading assignments, all the while wishing she was a better dancer and knew how to attract boys like Jorge Bacardi.

Certain memories can still trigger hot shame and aching regret. The Cuban Missile Crisis is one of them. The United States and the Soviet Union were engaged in what was called the Cold War. A month after I started college, the US government discovered that the Soviets were constructing missile launching sites in Cuba and secretly shipping missiles to the island. No way was our government going to tolerate Soviet nuclear weapons pointed at us from a communist-leaning country a mere ninety miles away. What followed was a high-stakes confrontation between the United States and the Soviet Union.

Better-informed and engaged students gathered in the student union, anxiously following the television news. As missile-laden Soviet ships approached Cuba, our government set up a blockade. Neither side would back down. Things were rapidly escalating out of control, and nuclear war was becoming a real possibility. For two weeks, the world was riveted to the unfolding showdown. Meanwhile, I was in the library anxiously writing my first term papers, completely unaware of what was going on. My ignorance about this critical event became emblematic of *all* the ways I'd been out of it during that time, surrendering my attention to the requirements of others.

Several guys fell in love with me; I was clueless. In keeping with the norms of the 1950s and early 1960s, my parents' expectations were simple: do well in school and remain a virgin until marriage. (I complied with the first; eventually I disregarded the second.) But at the time, my compliance was unquestioning. My own needs or wishes were never part of the equation. I was barely aware of *having* needs or wishes.

Looking back, it seems like I majored in holding back and missing out. No matter how much I grew and accomplished as an adult, I never completely made peace with my dutiful younger self. Now, I've come to Cuba to learn what I can about Cuban history. I am here to observe and listen and find out if it's possible to recover some of what I lost.

—

The host at my *casa particular*—one of the government-approved bed-and-breakfasts in the old section of Havana—carries my bag up a steep and narrow flight of stairs to my room. The room has grand floor-to-ceiling windows and doors. European influence is as evident here as it was in Colombia. The room is furnished with worn French provincial furniture. The bed has a padded pink satin headboard and pink chenille spread. As always, I'm most interested in the mattress. Ahh, my no-longer-youthful spine will be happy. The mattress is firm and comfortable.

My casa, in the old district of Havana Vieja, is just two blocks from the Malecón, the broad pavement that stretches for miles along Havana's waterfront. The Church of La Merced, built in the 1640s, stands at the end of my street. It will be the landmark I will use to help me return to the casa particular. Given my astoundingly poor sense of direction, a landmark is essential. I should be all right if I stay on the Malecón for my first glimpse of this island nation so revered by some and so vilified by others.

As I walk, I see kids playing soccer in the narrow streets and along the Malecón. I notice how many buildings need repair; sea salt and time have eroded them. I will soon learn that free education and universal health care are intentionally prioritized over infrastructure. It makes sense to me.

Passing a once-elegant hotel, I decide to stop and use its internet. At a whopping six dollars per hour, it is the most expensive internet service I've encountered anywhere in the world. When I discover that most Cubans earn about twenty dollars a month, I suspect these prices may be set this high as a way of limiting access to information about the rest of the world. I reluctantly pay the six dollars and email Charley to let him know that I've arrived safely.

The following morning, I am ready to locate and visit the Museum of the Revolution, hoping to fill in some gaps in my education. The museum does not disappoint. Dioramas, photographs, and written explanations provide the historical background I've been looking for. I learn about Castro's motivations for joining with others to overthrow the Batista government. The buildup to the revolution spanned my childhood and adolescence, from 1953 to 1959. Under Batista's rule, the obscenely rich became even richer. Money flowed to Americans doing business in Cuba, and the Mafia found a warm welcome. All the while, the rest of the population was falling into ever more desperate poverty.

In the museum, I move from room to room studying the photographs of Fidel Castro and reading the captions. What a powerful story they tell. When I come to a display case containing the radio Che Guevara used in the jungle, I stand there for a long time examining it. I can imagine Castro and Che and their compatriots listening for the crackling sounds of incoming messages and sending back their replies. I can also visualize the crackling tension among the rebels as they wait in their hideout for the signal to advance. This old, battered radio, more than anything else in the museum, brings the Cuban Revolution alive for me.

Now I have new questions. In the few days since my arrival, I've grown curious about the intense idolization of Castro and others who led the revolution. I am puzzled by the frozen-in-time quality of that reverence. After all, the revolution happened nearly a half century ago. The Bay of Pigs and the Cuban Missile Crisis are far in the past. The museum's propaganda—and the signs and banners I see along Havana's freeways—glorify Castro and give the impression that he is readying his country to resist another invasion.

Exiting the museum, I hail a taxi and step into what looks like a large yellow egg on three wheels. Unique to Havana, the egg-taxi feels a little tippy, but it gets me to my destination: the Casa de la Música. I enter the dark cavern of a dance hall where couples are moving fluidly to vibrant salsa music. A Canadian woman who is in Cuba for a week to learn salsa is enthusiastic in her praise. "Dancing with my Cuban partner is like dancing with liquid gold."

I listen to the music and think lovingly of my salsa-dancing daughter. Someday, I'm going to bring her here. But right now, I am on my own, and all I feel is self-conscious. Will I *ever* learn this dance? My hip is already aching after only a few minutes spent dancing alone in a dark corner of the vast venue.

Soon I leave and walk back toward the Church of La Merced in the rain. It's getting dark, and I feel sad and discouraged by the narrow streets with their potholes and puddles, the buildings with their chipped paint and cracked facades, the damp laundry hanging from wrought iron balconies, and the tired-looking old women leaning over those balconies. I'm feeling weary and lonely and inexperienced. I'm still confused by Cuba's two currencies. There are national pesos for Cubans, who earn incredibly low wages, and more expensive convertible pesos called CUCs for foreigners. To my inexperienced eyes, the bills and coins of both currencies look exactly alike. Even though I'm hungry, I am timid about going into restaurants till I've figured it out, so I buy snacks at a tienda and settle into my room with a good book.

Several days into my stay in Havana, rested and feeling more confident, I arrange to swim in the pool at the once-resplendent Hotel Nacional. The hotel was formerly a meeting place for the Mafia who ran a lucrative casino business in Cuba until Castro took over.

After swimming, I stroll the hotel grounds and discover a series of trenches and a small bunker. I've never been in a military trench, and as I walk through the labyrinth, I can just barely see over the top. The bunker is a tiny museum with memorabilia from the 1960s. There are photos of Che Guevara, Fidel Castro, and John F. Kennedy. I am startled to learn for the first time that after Castro's successful revolution, he initially approached the United States government for aid and support. When he was rebuffed, he turned to the more responsive Soviet Union.

Even forty years later, it is a relief to be informing myself. It's as if I brought my sixty-two-year-old self here to guide that frightened freshman: *You are in college now. You get to decide for yourself what is important. It's OK to close your history book and join your classmates who are watching and discussing the history being made right now.* As I walk through the dry trenches with my imagined younger self, I feel capable and content.

I've been in Havana for nearly a week. I'm glad to have visited the museums, but I haven't yet found a way to connect with Cubans in Havana. Where are the warm, happy people I came here to meet? I certainly don't see them as I walk the narrow streets of Havana Vieja with its potholes, mud puddles, and decaying buildings. Apparently, Havana has pleasanter neighborhoods and a lively university, but I haven't ventured far from my casa. I am quite ready to leave the capital and search for a smaller community.

The one I choose is Viñales.

Viñales is accustomed to visitors. My homestay, recommended by another traveler, is one block from the calle principal. Almost every house on the street has a little emblem indicating it as a casa particular. Names such as Villa Rosario and Casa Consuela are brightly painted on the houses themselves. I am staying at Villa

Lioska with a married couple and their two young sons. My host, like many people born in the 1960s and '70s, has a Russian name. However, unlike most Cubans, Lioska speaks quite good English. As she prepares dinner on the night of my arrival, I take out my kid kit and start to play globo-fútbol and frog-mitt baseball (a fuzzy ball and two Velcro mitts in the shape of a frog) with six-year-old Lazaro, nicknamed Chen, and four-year-old Lionel, called Chon. When our games wear me out, we go inside and make art projects using inked rubber art stamps with images of animals and insects. Soon Lioska calls us in to a bountiful, savory dinner of chicken, yucca, potatoes, rice, beans, potato chips, salad, fruit, and bottled water.

At first, I am bothered by the casa's mosquitoes and the neighborhood's crying babies, shouting kids, motorcycles, and roosters. But a good night's sleep works its magic, and by morning, I am quite glad to have found this lively family of four.

While we're playing globo-fútbol on the porch, Lazaro starts sneezing. Lioska informs me, "My son's nose is a very reliable weather predictor, and his sneezes mean rain is on the way. I've heard there's a bad storm blowing in from the direction of the United States." Sure enough, the following morning, I wake up to clouds and rain.

Hungry for physical activity, I book a hike despite the rain. Our guide shows us the strange outcroppings called *magotes*, and he takes us to a tobacco-drying barn, where he explains how cigars are made. When I return to the casa wet and bedraggled, Lazaro is on the sofa doing homework with his mom's help. At six, he is reading and learning to write in cursive. I invite him to read to me, and I'm amazed as he confidently sounds out the words. Not only is Cuban education available and free; if Lazaro is representative, it must be excellent.

Chon wants to make insect designs using the rubber stamps. A somewhat wild youngster when he's outside, Chon suddenly becomes a focused and industrious artist. I ask Lioska to remind me of certain Spanish words. I remember *abeja* (bee), *rana* (frog), and *mariposa* (butterfly), but I need help with "dragonfly."

"*Cigarro*," says Lioska.

I clarify the question. "*No, el insecto. En ingles, se llama* dragonfly."

"*Sí, en Cuba se llama cigarro*," Lioska repeats, and she points out the long, narrow body that—if you happen to be Cuban—looks a lot like a cigar. I stifle the impulse to laugh. Then I realize it's a wonderful example of how culture influences language.

Lioska is enthusiastic about the inflatable globe in my kid kit. She has wanted to teach geography to her boys. I am pleased to gift it to her. Maria, the children's grandmother, lives two houses away. She mentions that Lioska was a psychology major at university. That training is apparent as she interacts with her boys. With matter-of-fact neutrality, she informs Chon, her strong-willed four-year-old, "Children who don't sleep at nap time don't play with the globe later."

Although I'm disappointed about the rain, I am cozy in Lioska's house and content to write in my journal, read, and do laundry. By now, it's obvious to me that I flourish in the company of loving, happy families. One of the things I'm discovering on this journey is that for me, homes are safe places from which to explore and take chances. Perhaps I've been underestimating the importance of my own home as a potential nest and launching place.

There is live music in the Viñales plaza at night . . . every night. I walk the few blocks from Villa Lioska to the plaza, hearing the vibrant Latin music get louder as I approach the outdoor disco, the Casa de la Música. Shyly, I watch the band from the entrance to the gated venue; eventually, I pay to go inside.

I am aching to dance, but I really don't know how. I am alone, and no one invites me to dance. I am eighteen years old and a college freshman. I am two thousand miles from home, and I don't know anyone. I am at what's called a mixer, standing alone. .. so dreadfully alone. I'm scared of being ignored but even more scared of being asked to dance. No one asks. It never occurs to me that this might have something to do with the look of frozen terror on my face or the fact that I avert my eyes when anyone comes near.

I sit in the Cuban disco, surrounded by the music yet unable to release myself to it. I watch the Cubans dancing with abandon and skill. The band is good, and I briefly lose myself in the rhythm between upsurges of self-consciousness and longing to be one of the dancers. When I notice my unhappiness, I remind myself, *Hey, just enjoy the music. Nobody's watching you. Nobody cares if you dance or not.*

The band takes a break, and I head home down the dark streets with the salsa music growing fainter and fainter. I remind myself that I came to Cuba for music and dance. To succeed, I'll have to do what I couldn't when I was young: push through my self-consciousness and embarrassment. I am almost ready. I *will* learn to dance salsa.

In the morning, some Canadian women who've been staying across the street at Casa Marcella invite me to share a taxi back to Havana. I'm packed and all set to leave when Lioska mentions that there will be a little circus today in Viñales. Immediately, I begin my tortuous dance of indecision. *Should I go? I've agreed to share the taxi fare with the Canadians. Or should I stay? The sun is finally out; the children will be going to the circus. I always do better in small towns.* Impulsively, I apologize to my new acquaintances and return my fully packed bags to my room in Casa Lioska. The women are surprised, but they are gracious about it.

As soon as the taxi pulls away from the curb, I feel a gaping emptiness. I sit on the bed regretting what I've done. But I know myself: I'd feel this way whichever choice I made. How I wish I could be more decisive. For a little while, I just stay with the feelings and observe my critical self-judgments. Then I get up and walk the few blocks toward the Centro.

———

I enter the open door of a café. It appears empty. A guitar on the wall and a bar at the back suggest that this is a disco by night and a café during the day. A stocky man, most likely the owner, approaches me. *"Busco un hombre guapo que pueda enséñame bailar salsa."* What I'm attempting to say is, "I am looking for a handsome fellow to teach me how to dance salsa." After some appreciative laughter, the man beckons me over to the counter. While I stand there, feeling a little bit shy and a little bit brave, he makes a couple of phone calls, writes a name on a scrap of paper, and directs me to the plaza.

There are two teachers at the plaza; one is tall, the other is not much larger than me. Their class consists of one couple. The taller man indicates that I should join the lesson. He begins to instruct me, but I can't understand his coastal accent. After a while, we switch, and the smaller instructor becomes my partner. With effort, we can communicate. There is the rhythm and beat, the basic step, the open step, the *jiros* (spins), and the mysterious matter of knowing when it's time to change steps.

We practice for an hour. I want to learn what my partner is doing to circle his buttocks in that quintessential salsa way. Once I explain my wish, he places a hand on each of my hips and moves them for me. Feet flat, knees bent, hips moving firmly from side to side in rhythm with the beat, upper torso still. Plus, I'm supposed to *move*? *And* remember to breathe?

An hour later, the couple departs, and I continue for a second hour. The instructors take turns working with me so I can learn to follow different leaders. By now, I understand that my center of gravity needs to be lower. *Ayee!* I am using muscles that are accustomed to freeloading: the areas just above my knees and my *nalgas* (butt cheeks). I'm getting it! Encouraging smiles come from a Cuban man seated at one of the tables. After two hours, I am soaked with sweat, bright red in the face from the heat, nearly unable to move . . . and entirely happy.

I am amazed: my gimpy hip does not hurt, even after two hours of steady dancing. Keeping my feet flat and my weight low seems to offer protection. It's just possible that I really *am* learning to dance.

I return to Casa Lioska and lie down for a few minutes. After all that vigorous dancing, being vertical is exhausting. I wake up from a long nap and find out the boys and their dad have gone to the circus without me. Disappointed, I look for something to do that won't require the use of my legs. Lioska's front yard is full of weeds. I'm always happy playing in the earth, so I go outside and begin to weed. It feels good to sit on the ground. Four houses in a row belong to Lioska's family: parents, cousins, and an aunt. After some initial surprise to see me weeding, there is a small but noticeable shift among the neighbors in the direction of more openness. I guess the typical casa guest neither brings a bag of toys to play with the kids nor pulls weeds. But it works for me. I am so glad to be here and not in Havana.

"Is there a mirror I can take outside?" I ask Lioska one afternoon. I explain that I prefer cutting my own hair as I travel. "This way if I don't like it, I have only myself to blame." I sit on the floor of the front porch and snip away at my silver-tipped dark hair. From their respective porches, neighbors watch with curiosity as I approximate what I've seen my hair stylist do every six weeks for decades. Lioska's boys come out onto the porch and entertain themselves with the globo-fútbol. When I finish cutting my hair, I ask the older boy where his mother keeps the . . . I mime a sweeping action since I can't remember the word for *broom*.

From the porch next door, I hear "*escoba*" as a neighbor supplies the missing word and compliments me on a good haircut.

In the morning—a beautiful, warm Cuban morning—I am back for another salsa lesson in the plaza. "One-two-three; one-two-three." My instructor still has to count out loud to keep me connected with the beat while I move my feet. But I am learning to respond to the small signals he gives with his arms for turns or changing the step. My favorite is called *diga le no* (tell him no). It consists of a tiny foot stomp followed by a turn.

This trip to Cuba is a perfect example of forgetting and remembering. I was virtually at the point of loading my suitcase into a taxi to return to Havana when something tugged at my heart, urging me to remain in Viñales, to stay with Lioska's family a bit longer. Throughout our lives, we all tend to remember and forget, forget and remember. As soon as I found my way to a welcoming family and a comfortable venue for learning salsa, I remembered why I am here. And now I've not only found happy people in Cuba, but I *am* one of them.

CHAPTER 18

Viva Fidel

CUBA

*M*arcella talks so fast I can barely grasp a word she says.
A warmhearted doctor, she is the host of Casa Marcella,
right across the street from Villa Lioska. Today, when I come
home for lunch, Lioska tells me that her neighbor has just gotten
shocking news. Sofia, Marcella's twenty-three-year-old daughter
who studies at the university in Havana, has been missing for a
week. The parents are beside themselves with worry. The news
that their daughter is missing has hit the family *como una bomba*
(like a bomb), Lioska says grimly. I imagine how I would feel
if Mischa or Shahla suddenly disappeared without a word. I
would be devastated. By all reports, Marcella *is* devastated. *Una
bomba*, indeed.

After lunch, I walk to the internet café. While I wait for one
of the four computers to become available, I chat with the young
man behind me in line. Kirin is British, and like me, he is learning to dance salsa. He invites me to join him later today at the
home of his dance instructor, Juan Carlos. We meet as planned.
Juan Carlos is a good teacher. Kirin and I are practicing turns
when Juan Carlos's mother comes home. She is clearly upset, and

195

I hear her talking to her son in rapid-fire Spanish, something about a girl who has run away to the United States. I hear her say, "Marcella."

Ah, yes. This is life in a small town. Marcella's son and Juan Carlos are close friends. So, after our lesson, Juan Carlos walks me home, and we go across the street to speak with Marcella.

"Yes, I just got a call from a relative in Miami. My daughter is there," says Marcella, looking exhausted and slightly gray. "The important thing is that she is alive, and she is safe." Now her tone changes. "She doesn't even know English! She was such a good student. And she was just three months away from graduating with a degree in computer programming."

Later, Lioska will provide more details. "If Sofia had applied to emigrate legally after completing university in such a valuable field of study, the government would have refused her request." I wonder if this contributes to the regime's portrayal of the United States as an imminent military threat and a den of violence, drugs, and corrupting capitalism. Could it be part of an effort to stanch the ongoing brain drain from Castro's Cuba? After all, here is our country just a brief boat ride away, filled with so much of what Cuba lacks and what young people want: jobs, money, movies, electronics, new cars, novelty, and excitement.

Lioska tells me how frantically worried Marcella has been. Normally, Sofia comes home to Viñales each weekend, and they speak every day on the phone. For a week, no one could locate her. She was not at her house in Havana or with her boyfriend's family, and she hadn't been seen at school. When Marcella finally reached some of her daughter's friends, they said they'd over-heard her talk about going to Miami. As Marcella grasped the possibility that her missing daughter might be in a tiny boat on a huge ocean during the fierce storms of the past week . . . it is no wonder that she looked gray.

Finally, today came the call from the girl's aunt saying Marcella's daughter was with her in Miami. When Sofia came on the phone, Marcella said, "We've always been so close. Why didn't you talk to me?" Her daughter answered simply, "Because you would have said no."

"Is this sort of disappearance to the United States common?" I ask Lioska.

"In the small towns, it's not common. But it happens." And then Lioska tells me about the Cuban Mafia. "They pack too many people into small boats; they charge exorbitant fees. They might charge eight thousand dollars for their services!"

"Where does a young girl get that kind of money?" I ask Lioska.

"Someone brings the girl to her relative's door and says, 'Here is your niece. For eight thousand dollars, I will leave her with you. Otherwise . . .'"

By now, I've become almost certain that despite the rhetoric about Cuba's human rights violations and communist-leaning government, America's ongoing Cuban embargo is about financial gain and political power in Florida and Washington.

In addition to paying better attention to the news, I've grown more skillful at connecting the dots. Three years before my sabbatical, our administration further tightened its already strict policies limiting Cuban immigrants' ability to visit relatives back in Cuba. The established Cuban American community in Miami—an affluent and influential voting bloc—strongly favored this policy. Now, Sofia will not be allowed to visit her family in Cuba for three years! I am horrified by the inhumanity of this policy. My chest aches when I think about the impact on families in both countries.

This news is not only tearing up a family—it is tearing up an entire community. All day long, I see people come and go through the wrought iron gates of Marcella's house. It takes a village to raise a child, and this village is grieving.

Back at Villa Lioska, I think about the events of the day. I recognize another aspect of the drama of Marcella's daughter running away. Her actions are tacitly saying, "I love you dearly, Mom and Dad. But I've got to follow my heart. And my heart is taking me away from you. And that is my truth."

Once, long ago, it was my truth too. I can imagine Sofia struggling over wanting to choose what was best for her but also wanting to protect her parents from suffering. Nevertheless, she chose, and I admire her courage. When I left home, I faced a similar dilemma. How could I move across the country and have a marvelous time at college knowing I'd be triggering my mother's abandonment terror and depriving my dad of the roles he loved best: teacher, expert, unquestioned authority figure? My compromise was to go far away from my parents while leaving my exuberance and academic confidence at home. What a crummy compromise. My mother suffered from my departure anyway; it turned out that my father did too. Decades later, I would come across a little notebook in which he had written, "I am dealing with three deaths. In the last two years, I have lost my father and my sister. And now Leah is leaving for college. I know for a while she'll come home on vacations, but still, it feels like another death."

And now, here I am, traveling on my own for a year! Granted, it took four decades to accomplish, but it is still a triumph. For me, traveling without Charley means I finally believe I can follow my heart without causing harm to my husband or endangering our marriage.

Core conflicts never entirely go away. Yet here is proof that it's possible to tame our demons enough to coexist with an inner conflict rather than be crippled by it.

The band at the Casa de la Música is loud and satisfying. Kirin and I have come here to dance. He is leading well, and we are having fun. As I surrender to the music and take the risk of looking foolish, it seems that I too am leaving home in some more complete way. Not my home with Charley, but the earlier one from which I launched, perhaps incompletely. *I love you, Mom and Dad. And I feel for your needs and your yearnings, but my life must be filled with more liveliness: with music and laughter and friendship and play.*

Sometime after midnight, we walk home together. This small town in Cuba is far removed from my college campus, and I bear little physical resemblance to that anxious, pretty eighteen-year-old. But she is me, and I am she, and at last we are dancing!

On my final evening in Viñales, I am enjoying a delicious farewell dinner when suddenly I'm eating in the dark. Oh yes, I've heard that Cuba's electricity frequently goes down. Two more times during the evening, I'm treated to this quintessential Cuban experience. The second time, Lioska and I go out on the front porch and settle into two white rockers. Together we rock in comfortable silence under the stars. In the morning I'll be leaving for Trinidad, my next destination. If I can find a homestay this sweet, I will be fortunate indeed.

I break the silence to ask Lioska a question. "Do you like your life here in Cuba?"

"Very much," she replies simply.

Looking up at the starry night sky, I speak softly: "It seems like a very good life to me."

⎯⎯⎯

I am riding toward Trinidad in the comfort of a plush, air-conditioned tourist bus, a form of transportation few Cubans could afford. The tall bus provides a fine view of the giant banners strung from the overpasses that read ¡VIVA LA REVOLUCIÓN!

or *¡VIVA FIDEL!* Behind me, I hear voices speaking American English. I am surprised. I have been meeting Brits, Canadians, and many Europeans, especially Scandinavians. (It turns out that Cuba is a popular winter vacation destination for travelers from other countries.) But until now, I haven't encountered any Americans.

I twist around, and in the seats directly behind me are two passengers who appear to be a mother and daughter. I introduce myself and learn they are from Humboldt, California. Sandi is a nurse in her early fifties whose hippie past still shines through in her long blond braids, absence of makeup, and openness to the world. She has come to explore Cuba with her teenage daughter. Maya is tall and striking and looks like a supermodel, although in reality she is a bashful thirteen-year-old.

It is an eleven-hour bus ride from Viñales on the western side of the island to Trinidad on Cuba's southeast coast. However, it becomes a much longer ordeal when our bus gets a flat tire. Maya and Sandi and I alternately stand or sit on the curb, sweating in the hot sun for three hours, awaiting the arrival of a simple tool needed to remove the lug nuts from the wheel rim. In Cuba, a limited number of tools must be shared among many buses. When the bus carrying a socket wrench arrives, it is only a matter of minutes until the spare tire is in place and we are on our way. By the time we arrive in Trinidad, it is midnight and I am exhausted.

Ten and a half hours later, I wake up in my homestay fully rested. I dress and go into the kitchen. My host has her back to me when I enter the room. She turns from the stove and greets me. Eva looks to be about forty with light brown curly hair. She is polite but reserved. As she prepares eggs and toast for my breakfast, she asks what brings me to Cuba. In my halting Spanish, I explain that although the US government doesn't allow travel to Cuba and might charge a large fine, I want to see and experience Cuba for myself. While I am eating, several people arrive: a housekeeper, Eva's sister-in-law, and a man I never quite identify. To each visitor, Eva repeats the same introduction. "The señora came here from the United States and risked a huge penalty in order to see the *real* Cuba." Clearly, it is my desire as an American to experience *la Cuba verdadera* that makes the strongest impression on Eva and others.

Trinidad is a compact colonial city and World Heritage Site. As I walk around the historical district with a little tourist map, I peek through window grates into a primary school, a preschool, and a maternity clinic. Leaving the Centro Histórico, I'm elated to find a café that has a fleet of computers with high-speed internet. How different from tiny Viñales! I eagerly send an email to Charley filled with affection and first impressions of Trinidad.

On my way back to my casa, I bump into Sandi and Maya. Their homestay is close to mine, and we meet up in the late afternoon to stroll the Centro Histórico together. Music from the street draws us into a bar and music venue. Sandi and I each order something called *canchanchara*. Almost immediately, the concoction of rum, lime, club soda, and honey takes effect. Drinks in hand, we listen to a band play traditional Cuban music. The guitars and maracas and bongos are familiar, but the claves (a gourd played with a stick) and guiro (a kind of scraper) help create that Caribbean sound.

The more I sip my drink, the more I feel the music's rhythm inside my body. The lead singer's smile is like sunshine. My delight must be apparent because one of the young band members takes a break and invites me to dance. Later, Maya will take a photo of me sitting between two beautiful musicians, the three of us snugged up and smiling.

Trinidad is living up to its reputation as a city flowing with music. Later, walking through the *centro*, we follow the sound of violins to an outdoor venue where a group of female high school violinists are giving a performance of classical music. Evidently, supporting the arts is another priority in Cuba; the government

202 | MY MARRIAGE SABBATICAL

sponsors musical training for talented students like these young women in their long black dresses, holding their string instruments erect and playing their hearts out. Embraced by the balmy evening, the music, and new friends, I look up at the profusion of stars and think, *Here I am in a Spanish-speaking country where I can't understand most of what's being said; I'm in an unfamiliar city at night; I am staying with people I don't know . . . and I feel just fine.*

———

I tell Eva I'd like to take salsa lessons while I'm in Trinidad. She arranges for an instructor to come to the house and recruits her twenty-year-old nephew, Ramon, to be my dance partner.

Each day, Ramon comes by at salsa time. After three lessons, Eva suggests that he take me to the Casa de la Música to dance. "Don't pick up his bad habits," my instructor cautions me. With an edge of contempt in her voice, she adds, "He has the dancing style of the streets."

The dancing style of the streets seems to suit me. Amazingly, I can follow Ramon's lead *and* understand his Spanish. The outdoor salsa venue in Trinidad is much larger than the one in Viñales. In addition to the main stage, wide stone steps lead from the central square to the street above. On several landings, terraces extend out from the stairway in each direction. We start to dance on one of the landings. My kind young partner reminds me not to *saltar* (bounce) when I get excited.

After a while, Ramon guides me to a quiet terrace where we are tucked away behind some planters. I am relieved; I don't need the added challenge of dancing on cobblestones. When I thank him, Ramon explains that he chose this location to avoid being hassled by the police. They are constantly on the lookout for *jineteros*, local hustlers who offer themselves as escorts to female tourists. If we are asked, I am to say that he is a family friend.

"*No problema*," I readily agree. I know my Spanish is not up to the task of explaining to the authorities that I am a *jinetera*, and *I* have solicited *him* as a dance partner.

———

One afternoon, Eva and I find ourselves alone in the house. I have hardly seen her nine-year-old son, Alvaro. I inquire if he is off with his friends. He is indeed.

"How is that for you?" I ask.

"Sometimes it is boring to be alone in the house."

"Yes, I can understand. When my two children left home, I got lonely and depressed." Eva shares that she became quite depressed when they bought this house a few years ago and had to move a few blocks away from her parents and siblings. I am struck by the difference between Cuban and American ideas of "moving away from family." I visualize the row of houses in Viñales, where Lioska's relatives live side by side by side. Clearly, Eva would love such an arrangement. So would I!

On another day, Eva mentions that she previously worked in a maternity clinic.

"How is it that you went from working in a medical clinic to running a casa particular?" I ask.

Eva explains: "Even with both of us working, we had difficulty supporting our family on our salaries. Also, one of us being at home is better for raising our son."

Soon Eva and I are speaking openly about economic and cultural differences between the United States and Cuba. As we grow more trusting of each other and more adept at exploring complex issues in elementary Spanish, Eva reveals the full irony of giving up her job to host a casa particular.

"I loved my work, and I greatly miss being at the clinic," she explains. "My husband drives a bus, but he does not like his job. And it doesn't pay very much. We are better off running a homestay. My husband would prefer to run the casa, but it is expected that the wife will do it."

I'm intrigued that for all of Cuba's revolutionary and egalitarian ideals, it is still a traditional Latin culture. Eva stays home, bored to tears and wishing she were at work, while her husband reluctantly drags himself each day to his bus-driving job.

The paradoxes of Cuban life and culture continue to unfold. I came to Cuba to learn about its past, but I've become fascinated by its current contradictions and complexities. I am especially curious to understand the intertwined and ambivalent relationship between the United States and Cuba. I've read and asked questions and lived with Cuban families, but I know I'm only scratching the surface. In discussing politics, it's hard to differentiate facts from propaganda. I am not the only one confused by the Cuban government's propaganda. Eva, too, wants to figure out what is really going on. She looks to me for information. She wonders why the United States still wants to invade Cuba.

"I don't think that will ever happen," I respond. I resist the temptation to add, *Now if your country had oil, you might have something to worry about.*

Eva takes the conversation one level deeper. "My mother-in-law can't get over the fact that a married older woman like yourself would go traveling alone. She asked me, 'Why would anyone do that?'"

Her candid question deserves an authentic response, so I do my best to explain. "I didn't want to travel alone, but my *esposo* said he couldn't leave his work for such a long time. So, if I really wanted to visit and understand the world, it meant I must go by myself. To travel alone is a kind of *prueba*, a test. I get to practice being on my own after thirty years of always being part of a couple."

In the process of answering her question, it dawns on me why I always speak in such slow, halting Spanish. While I'm talking to Eva, my mind is racing ahead, rummaging through my meager Spanish vocabulary for the simplest words to express what I want to say. I console myself that I'll grow more fluent over time. (It will turn out that I'm dead wrong, but fortunately for my endeavor, I don't know that yet.)

Eva nods with understanding. She has an intelligence that's broad enough to span cultures, even though she has never been outside Cuba. She always remembers to speak clearly and slowly, a sure sign of cross-cultural sensitivity. I appreciate that she is patient and interested enough to overcome the language barrier. Our exchanges are deepening my understanding of *la Cuba verdadera*.

———

I am back in Havana. The month has flown by. In three days, I leave for Guadalajara, Mexico, where I will learn how to teach my own difficult language to non-English speakers.

I am down to my last few Cuban dollars. ATMs do not exist, and American dollars are not accepted in Cuba. I want to exchange my ticket to an earlier flight, but the change fee—the equivalent of twenty dollars—will leave no money for dinner. I change the ticket and dine on popcorn and water. I want to bring CDs of traditional salsa music to Shahla and Mischa, but if I do, I won't have money for a taxi. I buy the music and walk the several miles to my homestay, ending up sunburned and thirsty.

When I mention this to my English-speaking host, she responds unsympathetically, "This is daily life in Havana. I have ten pesos; the question is not 'Will I buy the perfume or the powder?'" She touches first her wrists and then her cheeks to illustrate. "It is 'Will I buy soap, or will I buy food?' *Now* you are living like a Cuban."

While I don't like the fear of running out of money, I feel a certain amused pride that I've successfully immersed myself in Cuban culture, albeit in this unintended way.

———

I arrive early for my flight to Guadalajara and wander through the Havana airport, feeling relaxed and peaceful. Looking at the enticing Cuban travel posters on the walls, I reflect on my month in Cuba. I think about the museums in Havana, and Villa Lioska, and my dance lessons in Viñales and Trinidad. I muse about my travel companions Sandi and Maya and the shocking disappearance of Marcella's daughter. And I contemplate the signs I saw everywhere in Cuba, the ones that said *¡Viva Fidel!*

In Viñales, a crudely painted *¡Viva Fidel!* sign was nailed to a tree on my route from Villa Lioska to the Centro. Another, located on a street corner a few blocks from my casa, read *¡Viva la Revolución!* Initially, they served as useful landmarks to help me find my way home at night. On the way in and out of Havana, I remember being surprised by the enormous banners stretched across freeway overpasses.

¡Viva la Revolución! *Why is the revolution of a half century ago being treated as if it were a present-day event?* ¡Viva Fidel! *And why do I keep thinking about those signs?*

Fidelidad means "faithfulness." In addition to its intended meaning (*Long live Castro*), the slogan *¡Viva Fidel!* holds a very personal message for me: *You kept the faith!* Yes, during my time in Cuba, I've been true to myself by keeping some long-ago faintly remembered promises.

In Havana, I faithfully learned all I could about Castro's revolution, the Cuban Missile Crisis, and the ongoing rivalry between two Cubas: the one on the island of Cuba and the other in Miami. *¡Viva la fidelidad!*

In Viñales, I trusted myself when I chose to stay in a small town where I could make friends and learn to dance. Bearing witness to the drama of a young girl's loyalty conflict and her brave decision was a bonus. It helped me reach into the past and connect with my earlier self—the teenager who had put her parents' needs ahead of her own. Oh, how she'd wanted to let loose and surrender to that 1950s rock and roll. In both Viñales and Trinidad, I immersed myself in music and dance. *¡Viva la fidelidad!*

Coming to Cuba provided a fresh chance to see history in the making. Cubans are increasingly curious about the outside world. They want to explore it; they want to know about other political and economic models. But Cuba's once-revered Father of the Revolution seeks to maintain authority long after it is needed to fight a revolution and long after such tight control is in the best interest of the Cuban people. The frustration is most clearly visible in Havana, where young people feel that national and local authorities are holding them back. Still, most Cubans love their island. Many are torn between staying or leaving. What a difficult choice!

Some choices beg to be both-and. Either-or is too painful. Surely Sofia must be aching to move freely back and forth between her career opportunities and her family. Charley and I have used our freedom to travel and return, to grow comfortable being together and being apart. When I think about it, I feel like one lucky woman.

Standing in line waiting for my flight to Mexico, I overhear two women speaking English just in front of me. Two more Americans: another mother and daughter.

"Where are you from?" I ask.

"Brooklyn," the daughter responds. "My mom's still there, but I live in Puerto Vallarta now."

"I'm on my way to Mexico for a month," I explain. "I hope there won't be any more surprise taxes before we get on the plane.

I just donated the last of my Cuban money to the women running the gift kiosk over there."

"We can always help you out if there are," says the daughter.

Ah, yes. This is what people don't realize when they imagine traveling alone. There is camaraderie among international travelers like the fraternity of Harley riders or the bond among dog owners.

For a solo traveler, the goal is to plan well and take care of oneself. Still, things happen. In Guatemala, I learned that *alone* was just an idea. Today, the Brooklyn woman's comment reminds me that even *on my own* is just an idea. I know I can count on Charley from afar. And nearer at hand benevolent strangers have a way of showing up just when we need them.

CHAPTER 19

Love and Loss

ARIZONA and GUATEMALA

"*Leah—it's time to come home.*"
My brother's email finds me in Guadalajara where I'm learning to teach English to Spanish speakers.

"*Mom has stopped eating and is failing fast.*"

I am astonished at how quickly I am on a plane headed to Tucson. In a matter of hours, I am kneeling at my mother's bedside, smiling into her eyes. Although she is no longer speaking, her responsive smile is acknowledging and reassuring. When my mother is awake, she looks at me lovingly while I caress her face or stroke the paper-thin skin of her hand. I quietly sing Threshold Choir songs to her. "You are loved, deeply loved . . ." and "I am sending you light to hold you in love."

I call my children and advise them to fly to Arizona so they can say goodbye to their grandma. I call Charley as well, and he promises to come as soon as he can get away.

After a while, I notice something. Whenever I say, "Mother, I love you," she smiles. But when I tell her, "Mother, I've always known how much you love me," she positively beams. Clearly, it means the world to her that I have recognized and taken in her love.

Charley flies in for a few hours to say his goodbye. My son and daughter arrive the following day in the early afternoon. They come bravely over to their grandmother's bedside. "Hello, Grandma," they say. My mother opens her eyes, and for the first time since my return, she speaks. In a warm, clear voice, she says, "Hello, darlings." These will be her last audible words.

Mother lives for another four days. Soon after the children depart, she begins the labored breathing known as a death rattle. Until now, I didn't know that this rasping breathing could go on for days. Over the weekend, I sleep on the floor next to her bed. My mother is no longer conscious.

The hospice nurse and our caregiver arrive at 9:00 a.m. on Monday. While they gently wash her, I stand on the other side of the bed, watching her face. Soon, quietly, she stops breathing.

As my mother's face and arms grow cooler, I reach under the covers to find the still-warm place near her heart. I know from my father's death that I must savor this mother-warmth now, for it will drain away in a matter of hours. My hand brushes lightly past the round underside of her breast. It feels so very much like my own. I remember crying against those soft breasts as a child. I remember looking at her tearstained dress and saying, "Oh, Mommy, I've gotten you wet." And I recall my mother's comforting reply: "That's what bosoms are for."

My mother's body is flown to the East Coast to be buried next to my father's. I fly east with her wedding ring in my purse and slip it back on her finger just before her burial. I know how much that ring and the security of her marriage meant to her. As I watch the wooden casket being lowered into the ground, my haze of protective shock suddenly ruptures, and I experience a moment of unprotected horror. *That's my mother you've got in that box!*

I think about my parents' tender sixty-two-year marriage with its amazing affection and apparent absence of disappointment, resentment, or anger. Their marriage was the obvious centerpiece in my mother's life and the secret treasure in my father's.

My own marriage to Charley feels so different. It is very authentic and solid, but kind of rough-and-ready. If my parents' marriage were dressed in elegant formal attire—I envision a floor-length ball gown of soft satin with long white gloves—our marriage wears cowboy boots and rides on horseback. There is some mud on the soles of the boots. And the horses need combing, but they can gallop fast, and they don't get tired. Occasionally, they stumble, but they always manage to catch their balance.

Back in Arizona, my brother isn't ready to dismantle the home where he stayed and cared for our mother. "I'd like to have the house to myself for a month. I need time to walk the halls and grieve." We agree that I will go away and return in a month. *What do I do now?* At first, I am at a loss. Then it comes to me. Guatemala was to have been my final destination after completing my English teacher training in Mexico. I already have a return ticket from Guatemala to San Francisco. If I buy a one-way ticket to Guatemala City, I can end my sabbatical where I originally planned.

———

I arrive in Guatemala in the late evening without a place to stay. I inquire at the airport, and soon I'm settled in a small, comfortable hotel five minutes from the terminal.

"My, you have become a relaxed traveler," Charley comments when I email him to tell him of my safe arrival.

In the morning, I call the Hostal el Montanes, hoping they will have a room available. Letty answers the phone.

"Doña Letty . . . ?" I begin.

"Doña Leah!" she exclaims.

It has been a full year since my visit, and yet, amazingly, Letty recognizes my voice. Best of all, there have been a couple of cancellations, so there *is* room at the hostel!

Excitement fills me as the shuttle bus crests that last hill into Antigua. I hadn't realized how emotionless I've been since my mother's death. Letty opens the front gate of the hostel and takes me in her arms. Luis gives me a bashful hug.

"I promised you I would come back," I tell my young friend. Luis has grown and matured. He has thinned out a bit; he adores *fútbol* (soccer), and he rides his bike over the cobblestone streets of Antigua. He informs me that he now has *bastante amigos* (loads of friends).

The hostel is as immaculate and beautiful as ever with the same plants, gleaming floors, rustic furniture, and colorful wall hangings. My favorite double bed is waiting for me upstairs. I shiver with delight as I set my suitcase down in the room. I smile at the familiar bedspread: burgundy flowers against a dark green background. It feels like coming home. I love that I now have so many places that feel like home.

Nothing can compare with the music of the birds around Antigua in the mornings. Their abundance and the intensity of their singing stand in sharp contrast to the relative sparseness of songbirds in the Bay Area.

On my first morning back at the hostel, Letty has courteously set a place in the dining room for my breakfast. I pick up my placemat and silverware and carry them into the kitchen. Letty smiles, and Luis is delighted. Letty makes scrambled eggs, coffee, and ripe papaya. The fresh eggs have so much flavor; they are just as I remember.

Letty not only recognizes my voice; she also remembers that I only drink half a cup of coffee and like Diet Coke in the afternoon. Carmen says Letty remembers all their guests. What a remarkable example of focused attention.

After breakfast, I prepare to walk over to First Street. It has been raining, and Letty warns me to be careful. If cobblestones can be treacherous, wet cobblestones are even more so. My first stop is the café/bookstore. I like the owner, a hip thirty-something expat from the United States. When I enter Café No Sé, John greets me. "Where the hell have *you* been?" When I tell him, "Bali, Java, Singapore, Costa Rica, Colombia, Cuba, and Mexico," he replies, "Where can *I* get a job like that?"

Next, I visit Ignacio Ochoa, the energetic director of Fundación Nahual. When we met last year, the former Jesuit quickly grasped the potential in a disaster workbook for children. At that time, I told him about an American NGO that might provide more copies if he wanted them. Ignacio followed up on my suggestion, and in response, the organization printed and shipped twelve hundred copies of *Mi Historia de la Tormenta Stan*. Ignacio recruited and trained teachers in the affected communities near Antigua. Now, he invites me to meet with some of the teachers who've used the therapeutic workbooks in their classrooms.

When I enter the Fundación Nahual offices a few days later, Ignacio and six teachers are seated around a table. "Would you like to see some completed workbooks?"

"*Por supuesto*" (of course). The outlined coloring book pages have now been filled in. Looking at them, my project comes to life. I can envision the children sitting at their desks, drawing. I can easily estimate their ages. The drawings in some work-books are neatly colored within the lines; these must be the older children. In others, I find the crayoned scrawls of younger chil-dren. In a different section of the workbook, the children have answered specific questions with drawings of their own. "This is my family"; "This is me during the storm"; "Here is the sad-dest or worst thing I saw"; "Here is the best thing I saw." Their stick figure drawings with speckly raindrops and horizontal trees convey shocking events and intense feelings.

The teachers clearly enjoy sharing their experiences. "We had the children fill them out over a number of weeks." "Compared with children in other classes, the ones who used these workbooks are calmer and more focused at school." "Their parents say they are sleeping better and seem much less frightened than before."

I can hardly believe what I am hearing. Yes, this was the intent of the psychoanalyst who designed these materials. And of course, it was my hope. Still, I am amazed.

At this moment, an Israeli volunteer enters the room to speak with Ignacio. He gets up and quietly carries on a lengthy conversation with her—in perfect English. Oh, my goodness! Last year, while I groped for my dictionary and did my best to make myself understood, this patient man, appreciating my valiant efforts to communicate in his language, never let on that he could speak English. This is not just a former Jesuit. This is a saint!

———

I am ready to visit my other family in Santiago Atitlán. Near the dock in Panajachel, the boatmen shout out "Santiago, Santiaaaago." I eyeball the lake. There are afternoon waves but no whitecaps; the smaller, faster *lancha* will be fine. An experienced commuter now, I sit near the back where the boat is more stable. When we land, a passenger hands my suitcase off the boat, and I roll it up the steep hill. My family's street is now paved. How wonderful.

After some welcoming hugs, I ask Lolita about her dream of going to school to study English. She tells me about her mother's illnesses. "The medicines she takes for high blood pressure and osteoporosis are very expensive. So instead, I am taking keyboard lessons." Without a hint of disappointment that her dream is out of reach, Lolita says, "Now I can also play the music when I sing with the children at Sunday school."

The sewing machine sits in its usual corner of the little store. I admire the huipil Chonita is working on. Even as I watch, the emerging bird becomes more vibrant.

In the evening, after supper, I join the sisters on the cement stoop of their tienda while we watch a torrential rain. The over-hang just barely keeps us dry, and we get giddier and giddier, laughing at everything and nothing. I love this family!

I accompany Lolita to the evangelical church, where she teaches a dozen children. Two teachers lead songs and tell stories while the children sit, squirming but otherwise compliant. When my host family brings me to attend an evening service, I will see many of these same children with their families. The church is a large cement room with folding chairs and a raised platform at the front. Some of the children smile, recognizing me from the morning. The older ones sit on folding chairs; the younger ones sit or stand near their mothers. For the entire two hours, all are silent and well behaved. There is no whining or crying, only occasional quiet interchanges among siblings. I imagine that in large families, children learn not to expect too much individual attention from their parents.

A mother with five little ones, all under age nine or ten, sits across the aisle from my host family. The woman holds a toddler, while a tiny girl not many months older suffers visibly from her desire to be held by her mother. She sits sleepily on a chair, nod-ding off and jerking awake, lip quivering.

I identify with this child, the only girl among the five. She clearly yearns for her mom . . . as I am longing for mine. Yet I know if I were to offer her my lap, she would refuse, finding no comfort there.

Finally, an older sibling points out the child's plight to their mother. At this point, I move across the aisle and gesture that I can hold the sleeping toddler. His mother hands him to me without a second glance. To my surprise, the little girl, who is dressed like a miniature adult in embroidered huipil and tiny woven skirt, does not crawl into her mother's lap and fall asleep. I suspect she doesn't want to squander even a moment of this precious opportunity. She perks up and leans over her mother's lap. Wrapped in her mama's shawl, she remains there, eating a snack.

I rock the sleeping toddler on my lap. It is delicious at first. However, after ten or fifteen minutes, the child's head grows heavier and heavier against my unsupported arm. Goodness, his mother must be strong. The baby flings a little arm in the air, and it lands inside the scoop neck of my black cotton travel shirt. Mothers and older girls seated nearby are smiling. After nearly an hour, the baby stirs and starts to wake. I shift his position so he is leaning back against my chest facing outward. He drifts in and out of sleep for a few minutes and then starts to turn his face toward me. I stand and return him to his mom before he awakens enough to realize he has been tricked. As I return to my metal folding chair, the women around me nod approvingly. I may be the only foreigner in the room, but there is a universal motherhood, and we all know I've acted skillfully.

To my surprise, the toddler—no more than eighteen or twenty months—stares at me with huge eyes from the safety of his mother's arms. Every time I look in his direction, he is staring. He eventually responds to my smiles with one of his own.

When the service is finally over, I approach the mother and tell her admiringly in Spanish, "You are very strong," gesturing that for me, her baby was heavy. Moms around us laugh; they had watched me shifting and struggling with the sleeping weight in my arms.

I walk home with my host family up the steep streets. Mama Mercedes falls behind; managing the incline is clearly an effort for her. Last year, she was carrying heavy baskets of wet laundry on her head. A year later, with no load, she struggles.

The next day, I return to the *albergue*. I am disheartened to see the same shelter still in the flood path of last year's mudslide, the same cubicles separated by plastic sheeting still housing the same people. Last night, violent rainstorms brought rivers of mud down from the volcano. How terrifying this must be to an already traumatized population. Seeing their poverty and deprivation is devastating. It appears that little has changed in the year since the mudslides. I learn that despite the obvious need, the disaster relief workbooks never reached the children in this shelter.

I am not only disappointed; I am puzzled. I spent weeks in Santiago Atitlán working within the community, engaging with organizations and individuals. I provided funds to print copies of the workbook. But apparently there was no follow-through, and the workbook was used very little in the indigenous villages around the lake. By contrast, I spent a single hour with Ignacio on my last day in Guatemala. He took initiative, obtained over a thousand workbooks, and put them to good use. What a tangible reminder that as with so much in life, our impact is not always what we think it will be.

I come back to my host family's house exhausted . . . positively deflated. I feel useless and ineffectual; I am angry and despairing and sad. I sleep and wake up still tired. I suspect that my sorrow over the plight of these abandoned indigenous families has opened the door to grief about losing my mother.

"Embrace the sadness," Charley tells me when I email him late at night. "It is letting you know you have lost something precious." I lean on Charley's wisdom around grief. My role model in learning to deal with loss was my orphaned mother. From my training, I know that children who lose a parent early in life are ill-equipped to do the work of grieving.

Lisa, a friend from home, is in Guatemala. She is in the process of adopting a Guatemalan baby. I meet her at a hotel, where adoptive parents come to spend a few days with their little ones while waiting for the government to complete its lengthy bureau-cratic adoption procedure. Lisa plays with Jardena in the hotel swimming pool along with dozens of other prospective parents and their Guatemalan babies. I notice that most of these babies have indigenous features.

During my visit with Lisa, I witness my friend falling pas-sionately in love with her four-month-old daughter. Jardena is an exceptionally pretty infant; she is placid and easy to love. Over their five days together, Lisa has become skillful at reading little Jardena's signals. She adroitly bathes and changes and dresses the baby, making her smile or squeal with joy. She sings her daugh-ter to sleep with lullabies. Then, at the end of the fifth day, she dresses Jardena beautifully, packs up her clothes and toys and formula, and goes down to the hotel lobby to return the infant to her Guatemalan foster family.

Jardena was relinquished for adoption on the day she was born. It was determined early on that Lisa would become Jardena's mother. DNA testing was done twice, confirming and reconfirming maternity. Nevertheless, the government routinely drags out the adoption process far longer than necessary. As a therapist and as a mother, I find this excruciating. At sixteen weeks, Jardena is open and ripe to bond with Lisa. Instead, she will go home with her foster mom. By the time the adoption is finalized, when Jardena is ten or eleven months old, she will be firmly attached to her foster family and they to her. That is precisely when she will be taken from a mother for the second time to go to an unfamiliar home in a country that speaks an unfamiliar language, to live with an unfamiliar woman who will be her mother. I am happy for Lisa and confident that she will be a fine parent, but I also know that disrupting a baby's firmly established attachment at such a crucial stage of development is hurtful and potentially harmful.

I can't help it. I am endlessly fascinated by the intensity of the loving bond and the helpless agony of its loss. I think how many films and novels portray the cycle of love, loss, and reconnection. Situations involving deep attachment and painful separation pull me as if by a magnet. They evoke my mother's early losses. They shine a light on my own vulnerability around separation. I've spent nearly a year apart from Charley, strengthening my ability to deal with separations and proving to myself that I have grown sturdier over time.

The hotel lobby at 6:00 p.m. is filled with clusters of adoptive parents, caregivers, and babies. The Guatemalan caregivers and the Americans sitting nearby listen with interest as I translate Lisa's questions and heartfelt expressions of gratitude to Jardena's foster family. They watch her hand little Jardena back to her foster mother, along with satchels of baby items Jardena will need for the next several months. After the baby and foster family depart, the onlookers collectively wince as they watch my friend fold up into herself on the sofa and slowly fall forward over her knees, sobbing.

———

By serendipity, I'm ending my sabbatical in Antigua just in time for Semana Santa. In the week leading up to Easter, throngs of visitors come to Antigua for its spectacular celebration of death and rebirth. The event features the creation of brilliantly colored *alfombras* (carpets) created from dyed sawdust, which extend all along the streets of the town.

Just around the corner from the hostel, neighbors are creating an alfombra in the road. The sawdust carpet has a pattern of sunflowers surrounded by an elaborate border. I watch in fascination as these once-yearly street artists lay down handmade stencils and fill the open spaces with various vibrant colors. One person is carefully spreading coffee brown into the oval stencil to make the center of the sunflower; others outline the stems and fill them with dark green sawdust; still others are adding light green leaves. My favorites are the bright orange sunflower petals. Lots of people are working simultaneously on the carpet that takes up most of the block.

I ask if Luis and I may join in, and we each receive a pail of sawdust and a stencil. Long planks resting on blue plastic milk crates straddle the width of the carpet. The planks allow us to reach the center of the carpet without disrupting the sawdust designs that have already been laid down. Luis is working on the border; I have a stencil and light green sawdust to make sunflower leaves. As I work, lying on my stomach on the board, tourists and Guatemaltecos walk by taking pictures. To one I remark, "*Está bien para el alma, pero mal para la espalda.*" (This is good for the soul but hard on the back.)

No matter how many repetitions we do, I never fail to be excited each time the last stencil is carefully lifted off to reveal a completed sunflower. We work collectively for many hours, finishing the carpet close to sundown. Throughout the town, residents of almost every street are creating alfombras.

The next morning, before the procession begins, Luis and I walk through the streets. We are part of the huge throng of tourists and Guatemaltecos admiring the vast quantity and originality of the alfombras. The colors are extravagant. I am thrilled by the intensity of the women's traditional clothing against the brilliance of the carpets' colored sawdust. The completed alfombras are works of art. Some are so long that ladders are set up at opposite ends to help viewers see the entire carpet. Still, I love our sunflower carpet the best. I feel fortunate to be a participant in Semana Santa rather than simply a tourist behind the lens of a camera.

In the early afternoon, Luis, Letty, and I stand on the corner near the hostel, where we can see our alfombra as the procession comes through. It is imposing. There are Roman centurions on horseback and men dressed in purple hooded robes carrying a massive cross. Mary rides on a float carried by dozens of women dressed in black who walk bent over from the weight of the enormous platform. The procession arrives on our street and tramples our creation.

As soon as the entourage has passed by, a huge truck comes through. Men with push brooms jump off and sweep up the sawdust that is now a random multicolored mix. They toss it onto the truck bed and move on to the next alfombra.

We worked so hard to complete our carpet on Thursday night, only to have it destroyed by the religious procession as it passes through the streets the following day. On Good Friday, those streets become holy ground. This tradition serves as both a religious offering and a tangible reminder of life's impermanence. For me, its meaning resonates deeply. I think about this fragile life. I think about my global families, and my own children—and the man I am about to return to. I feel grateful to have a partner who could understand what I needed. Charley knew that I was ready to become more open: open to the world and open to life.

I put my arm around Luis's shoulder, and we head back to the hostel. In the morning, I will be leaving Guatemala, my year of travel complete.

CHAPTER 20

Not Quite the End

*M*y eyelids flutter. Even before opening them, I know I'm not in my own bed. But it is wonderfully comfortable, and the sheets are silky soft against my skin. I take a deep breath, open my eyes . . . and there is Charley's face next to mine on the pillow. We grin at each other. Our smiles are mirror images of happiness and friendly collusion.

Charley is taking a six-month sabbatical!

We are in a bed-and-breakfast tucked up against Table Mountain in Cape Town, South Africa. After decades of hoping and suggesting and inviting and ultimately letting go, my travel dream has become Charley's as well.

———

When Charley first proposed taking a sabbatical, I was caught by surprise. "What!" I responded. "*What?*"

"Yes, I think I might like to take six months off from my practice to travel. With you, of course."

I was utterly dumbfounded. Here was Charley proposing what he had flatly refused to consider when it was *my* dream. When I was the one seeking companionship for a scary adventure. "When would you want to go?"

"In five years."

How impetuous of you, I remember thinking. What I actually said was, "Where would you want to go?"

"I'd like to go back to South America and study indigenous dreaming in the Amazon."

"Yes, of course I'll go. But frankly, I'm more interested in Africa than South America."

It was time for another negotiation.

It didn't take us long. We agreed to spend three months on each continent. Charley generously offered to visit "my" continent first.

I am now sixty-seven and Charley is sixty-five. Wherever we travel, I see the fact of our advancing age reflected in the reactions of others.

Africans are respectful of the elderly, but they are also matter-of-fact, even blunt, about aging. When we say goodbye to our favorite taxi driver on the way to the airport at the end of our month in Ghana, we thank him for his kindness.

"There were two reasons I wanted to help you," replies the goodhearted man. "I could see you didn't know where you were going. And also, you are old."

Charley and I are still getting over our amusement when we reach the departure gate for our flight to Tanzania. I hand my passport to the official. He looks back and forth several times from my passport photo to my face. "Yes, that *used* to be me," I comment cheerfully. Like many Ghanaians, English is not his first language. Smiling, he replies courteously, "Madam, I think that time is not on your side."

Charley and I stifle our laughter until we're on the plane.

The most amusing and playful encounter of all takes place on this same journey from Ghana to Tanzania. Our flight involves a long, tedious layover in Ethiopia. For hours, Charley and I sit in a massive, gloomy waiting area at the Addis Ababa airport. Because the building is still under construction, the vast room has cement floors, stark unfinished walls, and dim lighting. Row after row of hard wooden benches look like pews in an unfriendly church.

At midnight, Charley leaves to find something to eat, and I am sitting by myself. On the benches around me are throngs of Muslim families waiting for their flight to Riyadh, Saudi Arabia. Tired, restless children in front of me keep turning around to stare at my white face and uncovered gray head. *There's got to be a better way to amuse them.* Reaching into my pack, I extract a large finger puppet from my kid kit. It looks like a locust; it's about seven inches long and incredibly ugly. It has a leather face with protruding bug eyes, a black fuzzy thorax, and gauzy sheer wings. Its tail is a long, transparent green tube with an LED light in its butt. I slowly, slowly move it up the back of the long bench in front of me. As the bug crests the top of the bench, I straighten out my finger, causing its butt to glow a bright startling green.

The half dozen kids who have been watching me grow bug-eyed themselves. Over the next fifteen minutes, as I make the finger puppet light up and prance over the top of the seats, black-robed mothers smile, dozens of other children begin pointing and laughing, and some of the braver boys come over to touch the giant insect. With my encouragement, they stop hitting it and take turns stroking it gently. Soon a circle of eager young kids comes close. I tell them my name and point to them. One by one they respond: "Suleiman." "Ahmed." "Mohammed." Formal and serious, each one makes their introduction. By the time the flight to Riyadh is called, the waiting area is a sea of smiles, and the children depart in a chorus of "Bye-bye, bye-bye!" This brief cross-cultural encounter captures the essence of the person I wanted to be when I began my solo sabbatical and who I have become thanks to my travels with and without Charley.

In South America, we return to the jungle, where Charley initiates his dream research with the Achuar tribe, interviewing community leaders and indigenous healers.

Although there is lots to see during our travels on two continents, what I savor most is spacious time with Charley. In hotels or bed-and-breakfast accommodations, I read aloud to him—novels and books about the countries we're visiting—while we lie on the bed with our toes touching or our legs entwined. I am charmed by this transformed, affable fellow who is adventurous and at ease and seems fully present. I can't resist teasing him: "Please understand. I still love my husband. But I am *so* glad I decided to run off with you."

After three months together in South America, we arrive at the last evening of our journey. Charley and I are in Mexico, resting for a few days on our way home. We are walking on a quiet curving beach on the Pacific Coast. A dramatic sunset is painting itself across the sky, the impossible pinks and blues and oranges reflected in the ocean. We are eager to see our children and close friends. Charley is enthusiastic about returning to work. I have trepidations.

I think about those long, restless evenings at home, waiting for Charley. As the color fades from the sky, I wrap my sarong tighter around my wet swimsuit and share my concerns with Charley. "This has been a glorious six months. But I worry that once we're home, you're going to get too busy; I'm going to get lonely and resentful, and we're going to drift back into our old patterns."

Charley shakes his head. "Don't assume that. We don't know yet how we've been changed by this trip. We've learned a lot about ourselves and each other. I think it's going to make a difference."

I listen to Charley's optimism. I think how much easier it has become to feel proud of Charley when I am feeling capable and proud of myself. *Dare I be hopeful?*

In the morning, Charley wakes me, shaking my shoulder ever so gently. "Hey, sweetheart, it's time to get up and get dressed. We've got a plane to catch." I turn toward him and sigh. His forehead and balding pate have grown more suntanned with each passing day. Brushing my lips against that smooth, shiny surface, I breathe in his familiar scent. "OK, Charley, let's go home."

Epilogue

During my career as a psychotherapist, I worked with couples going through transitions. These included parents who were transitioning from the child-rearing years to living once again as a couple and long-married partners who were facing later life. Many of them felt unsettled. In certain cases, they were considering divorce. As I listened to their stories, I realized that these couples were seeking a breakup, not so much from *each other* as from stagnant or outgrown patterns of marriage. They were fighting for change! Underneath their struggles was the wish for a fresh and dynamic marriage, preferably with the same partner.

I, too, had been searching for change when I shook up our nest more than a decade ago. What neither Charley nor I realized when we agreed to be apart for a year was that we were in the process of reconfiguring our marriage. We were experimenting with a different version of matrimony, one that was flexible and spacious enough to support independent dreams as well as those we shared.

When I was in my late thirties, I visited a former college classmate who lived in Hawaii. Caroline and I had both married professionally ambitious men. We were caring for young children, juggling careers, and struggling a bit. As we sat together on a beach, each of us describing our satisfactions and frustrations with the spouses we had chosen, I turned to Caroline and asked, "Do you know any couples who have a truly gorgeous marriage?" I remember being startled by her response: "Yes, a few. But they're all over seventy."

At the time, seventy felt as far away as a distant planet. Who knew the mysteries of life on that planet? It never occurred to me that *I* would eventually become seventy. I was unaware that couples might continue to grow as individuals and partners all the way into and through old age. I had yet to learn that a good-enough marriage *is* a good marriage. I wouldn't have believed that with fewer hormones and more appreciation, lovemaking could remain just as satisfying—or even sweeter. And I certainly didn't foresee that I could remain in my own complicated marriage, confront many of the same difficulties and frustrations, and yet feel appreciative and mostly content.

But amazingly, it has happened. Our relationship is changing. Charley is working from home!

For the first time in our marriage, Charley's personal and professional life are in the same physical space. The deadly COVID-19 pandemic and the mandate to shelter in place were the catalyst for this change. Now, even though the worst of the pandemic is over, Charley is choosing to work from home two days a week. His professional meetings are scheduled mostly on weekends and take place remotely using Zoom. That means Charley is home for dinner *every* night! It turns out he loves having meals together. I love preparing them. Even though salons have reopened, Charley prefers the less professional haircuts I give him on our back deck. I enjoy playing with his hair as I groom it.

Thanks to our forced proximity, we are sharing more of who we really are. This intimacy, this willingness to be open and vulnerable, is what was missing. *This* was the source of the loneliness I felt but couldn't articulate.

Now, along with telling me about his day, Charley tells me when he's feeling proud of an accomplishment, or when he's dealing with some tricky issue within his professional community, or when he can use a hug. (Of course, it is a lot easier to be authentic with a wife who listens with genuine interest and fondness rather than irritation or unsolicited advice.)

Our house no longer feels like a lonely place. Although I barely see Charley during his eleven-hour workdays at home, I know he is nearby. On those days, his only commute is to the kitchen to grab a sandwich. Sometimes he comes up behind me and places the gentlest whisper of a kiss on a sensitive area at the back of my neck. When he finds the perfect spot, it invariably gives me shivers.

I think it always will.

A Guide to Conducting Your Own Couple Retreat

A couple's retreat is an opportunity for partners to set aside time and create private space to focus on their relationship, identify shared and individual dreams, and make specific plans toward realizing those dreams. They are designed for couples in stable relationships who want to strengthen their friendship, learn skills for collaborative decision-making, and support each other in fulfilling important aspirations.

For couples who are in considerable conflict or actively considering divorce, a self-guided retreat is not a helpful process. Individual therapy and/or couple counseling may be more effective in supporting the relationship or helping partners reach important decisions about it.

For those of you embarking on a self-guided retreat, I have provided a sampling of materials and instructions.*

A more complete set of materials, instructions and strategies for success are available on my website, www.mymarriage

---

*These materials are copyrighted and for personal, non-commercial use only. Any other use of these materials requires prior written permission from the author.

sabbatical.com. You can submit questions or comments there about the retreat process or about specific issues you and your partner are exploring.

On the website, there is also a photo gallery portraying the families and events I encountered in each country during my year of travel.

Starting exercise: Ten Things I Love about You

This is a simple but powerful warm-up exercise to begin your retreat. Individually, list ten things you love and value about your partner. Take your time preparing your lists, then read them aloud to each other. Read slowly so your partner can take in what you are telling them.

Satisfaction Scale

The scale on the next page provides a snapshot of each partner's current satisfaction with important aspects of their life. (10 is most satisfied; 1 is least.) Fill out the scale independently. The space provided for comments is for clarification, *not* for complaints or criticism. When you have both completed the scale, share and compare your responses. Low ratings or very discrepant ones in a given category may suggest topics to discuss during your retreat. For now, just listen. Do not debate or challenge your partner's responses.

Category	Score 1–10
FAMILY	
EXTENDED FAMILY	
LOVE/SEX	
HOME	
FRIENDS	
HEALTH	
MONEY	
WORK	
COMMUNITY/LOCATION	
LEISURE/FUN/TRAVEL	

Modified from the Happiness Scale in *The Working Relationship*, Lisa Stelk and Cheryl Newman, Villard Books © 1986

Comments and Notes

FAMILY

EXTENDED FAMILY

LOVE/SEX

HOME

FRIENDS

HEALTH

MONEY

WORK

COMMUNITY/LOCATION

LEISURE/FUN/TRAVEL

Discussion Questions

These questions can give you a starting place for some of the most important conversations you may have during your retreat. Listen to your partner's responses without debate or disagreement. If either of you feels triggered or senses defensiveness or distress in your partner, agree to set aside discussion of that topic and return to it later.

- What do I think is going well in our relationship?
- What might we want to change or improve regarding our relationship?
- What is one thing I wish I could discuss with you more openly, more comfortably, or more effectively?

Choosing Topics/Making an Agenda

Based on these exercises and conversations—and others described on the author website—jointly choose a manageable number of topics for the time you have available. Perhaps select a couple of major issues and several straightforward ones. As you gain experience and confidence using the retreat process, you may decide to increase the number of topics.

*Worksheets**

The worksheets for planning and problem-solving consist of a sequence of steps designed to effectively address a particular issue. Each topic to be discussed should have its own separate worksheet. Below, I've outlined the steps and included examples from negotiations that Charley and I had about my sabbatical.

1. NAME AND DEFINE THE ISSUE OR PROBLEM

Frame the issue or problem as a question in a way that promotes conversation and collaboration. Start with "How can we . . ." (Charley: *"How can we help you experience life in a different culture while also meeting my needs and protecting our marriage?"*)

2. DIAGNOSE THE ISSUE

Identify each partner's issues and concerns. Why is this issue especially important? Why is it a problem? What personal dreams might be embedded in this issue? (Leah: *"I've wanted to live and volunteer in other cultures since I was young. I still regret holding back. Traveling now would feel like I was being true to myself and would make me proud of who I've become."*)

Do not focus on solutions yet! This is a conversation, not a sales pitch. What needs, wishes, and concerns must be recognized and addressed before deciding on a plan? Your answers will be both practical and emotional. Brainstorm and write them down. (Charley: *"If we go together, I'm concerned about being away from my work for a year. If you go on your own, I am concerned about missing you and about long periods without sex."*)

What about this issue is already going well? (Both: *We know our marriage is sturdy enough to weather being apart.*)

3. DEVELOP OPTIONS OR POTENTIAL SOLUTIONS TOGETHER

What would success look like? Imagine it is a year from now and you are both proud of how you are dealing with this issue. (Leah: *I went by myself, and Charley has been fine on his own. We are proud of each other, and our marriage is still okay.*)

What are we doing differently? (Charley: *We're learning to be comfortable on our own. I'm taking better care of myself.*)

What additional information might be useful to reach a mutually satisfactory decision? (Both: *Clarify savings available for travel, identify fixed home expenses, calculate lost income if we both travel or if Leah goes solo, and estimate expenses for low-budget travel.*)

Brainstorm possible options or solutions. List all ideas. Do *not* debate or dismiss suggestions. (Both: *We could wait a few years to see if Charley might want to travel too. Take several short vacations. Accept that a year of travel isn't feasible. Decide that Leah will travel on her own while Charley continues to work.*)

4. DEVELOP AN ACTION PLAN
Select an option to try first. (Both: *Leah will travel on her own for a year.*)

What steps must be taken? Who will do what? What is the time frame? (Both: *Leah will give clients eight months' advance notice. Together we'll plan several reunions.*)

How can we support each other? (Both: *Leah will include Charley in the planning process; Charley will agree to have Leah's back during her travels.*)

5. FOLLOW UP AND EVALUATE
Set a date to review progress and put it on the calendar. This could be three to six months after a retreat, unless an issue is time-sensitive. (Both: *We'll take time during each reunion to discuss our satisfaction and deal with any problems that come up.*)

---

*This worksheet was modified and used with permission of Joel Schaffer, retired commissioner of the Federal Mediation and Conciliation Service.

Review each issue. What did/didn't you accomplish? Did you get the results you wanted?

Modify plans or choose a new strategy as needed. (Both: *Leah's difficulty with Charley's new relationship necessitates a revised agreement about sexual conduct while apart.*)

I hope this material is helpful, and I wish you a satisfying and successful retreat experience. Perhaps you will make it a yearly event!

Reader Discussion Questions

Since not all readers may be in relationships, you might also think about these questions in terms of a friendship or a past or envisioned future relationship.

1. What parts of Leah's story especially intrigued you? What could you most relate to?

2. This is a book about *integrity*, both in the sense of being true to ourselves and in the sense of wholeness—becoming fully who we are. How can we address our own needs and life dreams while also honoring the needs of our partner and our partnership? What might be some of the challenges to achieving this?

3. Has this book awakened in you an unlived dream or ambition of your own? (Yours may have nothing to do with travel; it may not entail any separation from your partner.) What is one specific step—perhaps a small one—that you can take in the direction of making this desire a reality in one form or another?

4. *My Marriage Sabbatical* demonstrates that you don't have to be a bold person to pursue a bold dream. Fisher describes her journey as an act of "shy courage." In what ways do you consider yourself courageous? In what ways do you believe you are not?

5. What are your reactions to Charley? Do your opinions change as the book progresses?

6. This book is an exploration of marriage in later life. What insights does the story offer about the changing needs of partners throughout the lifecycle of a long-term relationship? What might you now want from your relationship that is different from what you wanted or needed at earlier stages?

7. What do you think about this couple's negotiating process? How might you use some of these techniques to address important issues in your own relationship?

8. If you could ask the author one question, what would you ask her? What question would you like to ask Charley?

Leah invites you to reach out to her with these or other questions at her website: mymarriagesabbatical.com.

Acknowledgments

*W*hen you take fifteen years to write a book, you end up with a lot of people to thank. (I've calculated that in the time I spent working on *My Marriage Sabbatical,* I could have birthed nine elephants!) I am grateful to the many midwives who helped deliver this long-gestating memoir. Profound thanks to each of you—and to others I haven't mentioned by name.

To Brad Dessery for that 1970 postcard with its map to Panajachel and cryptic message: "Paradise is alive and well." To Sacha Kawaichi, my travel companion in Hawaii and in life.

To Elizabeth Fishel, in whose Wednesday Writers group I first imagined myself as a writer. Thank you, Elizabeth, for your steadfast encouragement and multiple thoughtful readings of this manuscript.

To Ricki Jacobs for consultation on closing a therapy practice with integrity.

Carol Jenkins: my profound gratitude for our deep conversations that led me to believe a good-enough marriage *is* a good marriage.

To Brooke Warner for your guidance in structuring and writing a memoir. To my Artists' Conference Network group for supporting and acknowledging one another's creative endeavors.

I am forever grateful to the friends who invited me to write at their dining tables during the years when I was more productive in their houses than my own: Judy Bloomfield (I loved our "Judy Tuesdays"), Helen Neville, Jean Rains, Chris Essex, Judy Scher, and Jill Targer.

Thank you, Helen, for repeatedly urging me to include a retreat guide and then partnering me in writing it.

I received valuable feedback and support from those who have read and reread my manuscript over the years: Elizabeth Fishel, Jamie Woolf. Helen Neville, Jean Rains, Phyllis Cath, Carol Jenkins, Judith Viorst, and Ann Kletz.

Special thanks to twenty-one longtime friends who agreed to let me read a chapter aloud to each of them so I could listen to the sound of the words and make small edits along the way.

Abundant thanks to my editing team, Joanne Hartman and Vicki DeArmon. Joanne, thank you for insisting that I commit to three themes and ditch the rest, for stepping in when I needed you, and for firmly declaring, "It's DONE!" Vicki, you were a splendid thinking partner. Thank you for keeping me organized, shortening and eliminating chapters, providing much-needed version control, and then declaring, "It's DONE!"

To the people at She Writes Press: What a brilliant idea to create author cohort groups— perfect for a women's press. I relied on this sisterhood of support as we moved through the publishing journey together. Brooke, thank you for skillfully orchestrating the publication of our books. Special thanks to Krissa Lagos and my project managers, Addison Gallegos and Shannon Green.

Thank you, Sarah Kolb-Williams, for your meticulous copyediting and amazing research. I never imagined that a relationship confined to the margins of track changes could become so warmly collaborative.

My appreciation to those who gave permission to use their materials in this book: Laura Fannon for her song, "My Grateful Heart;" Lisa Stelck for the Satisfaction Scale; and Joel Schaffer for ideas incorporated into the retreat worksheet.

242 | MY MARRIAGE SABBATICAL

Heartfelt thanks to all the families that hosted me on my travels. I've remained close to several: Hazel's family in Costa Rica, Letty's in Guatemala, my laughter-filled family in Santiago Atitlan, and my host family in Bali. To Paola, Luis, and Putu Lia: you are now grown, but I am still your global grandma!

I want to acknowledge California governor Gavin Newsom, whose mandate to shelter in place during COVID transformed my marriage.

Finally, I am grateful beyond words to "Charley," who stepped *wa*y outside his comfort zone in agreeing to my sabbatical. Thank you for your generosity in going along with a plan that involved long stretches of time apart. Thank you for your openness in supporting the writing of this book. It meant putting my efforts at creative expression and this book's potential to benefit other couples above your own predilection for privacy. I loved your whimsical working title, *Travels Without Charley*. And I marveled each time you said, "It's *your* book; write what you want." Just so you know, I think that a husband who genuinely wants to make his partner's dreams come true is quite a romantic fellow.

About the Author

*L*eah Fisher worked for thirty-five years as a psychotherapist, marital counselor, and corporate consultant. During this time, she brought her expertise to television programs including *The Oprah Winfrey Show* and *60 Minutes*, and to media outlets including *Newsweek* and *The Wall Street Journal*. Although Fisher is pleased with her professional accomplishments, she is exceptionally proud of exploring the world for a year on her own. She is a self-proclaimed "wild and crazy grandma" to four young grandchildren. She lives with her husband in the San Francisco Bay Area.

Author photo © David Burwen

Looking for your next great read?

We can help!

Visit www.shewritespress.com/next-read
or scan the QR code below for a list
of our recommended titles.

She Writes Press is an award-winning
independent publishing company founded to
serve women writers everywhere.